GW01605320

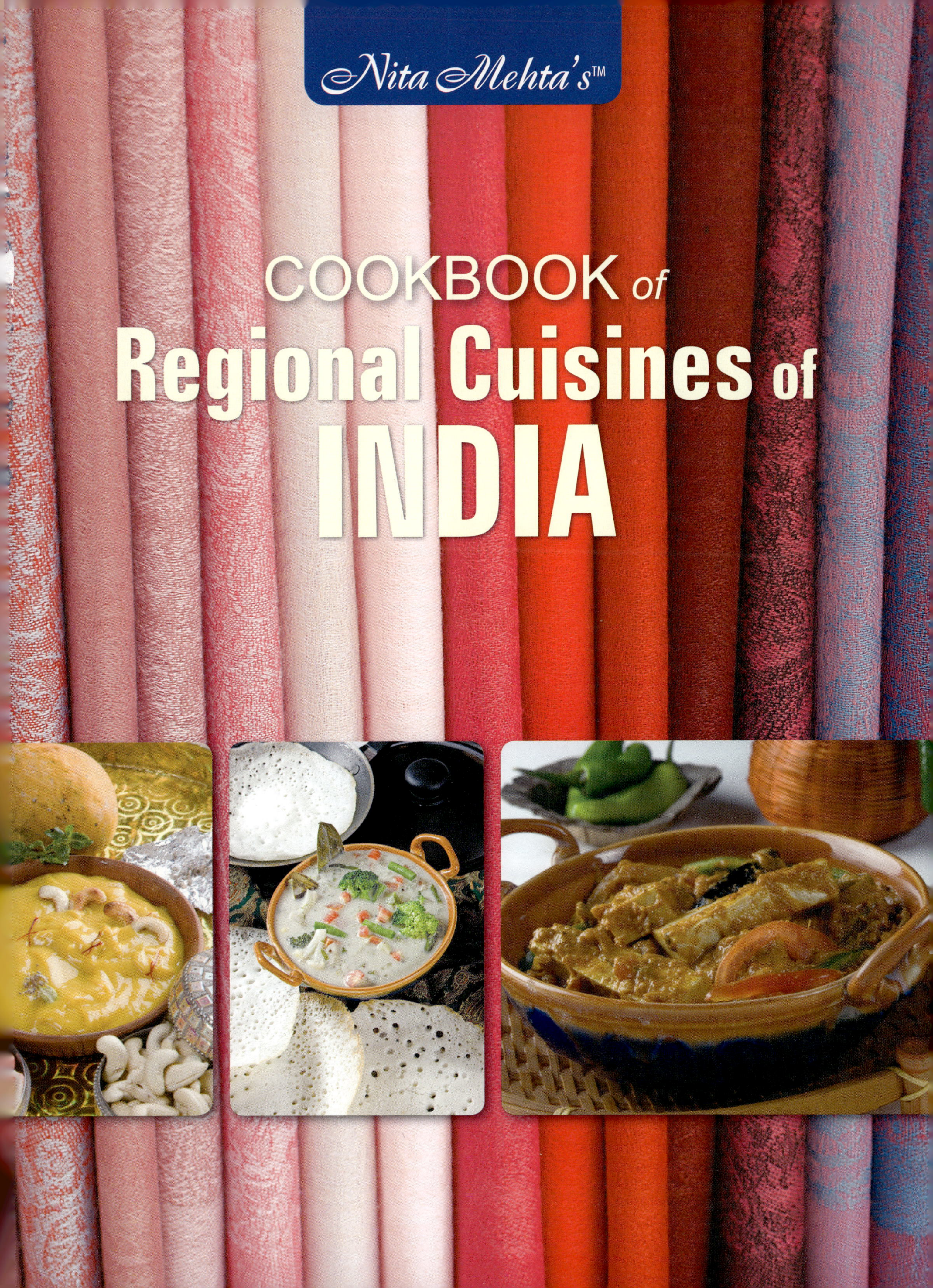
Nita Mehta's™
COOKBOOK of
Regional Cuisines of
INDIA

Nita Mehta's™

COOKBOOK of Regional Cuisines of INDIA

COOKBOOK of
Regional Cuisines of INDIA

Snab Publishers Pvt Ltd

Corporate Office
3A/3, Asaf Ali Road, New Delhi 110 002
Phone: +91 11 2325 2948, 2325 0091
Telefax: +91 11 2325 0091
E-mail: nitamehta@nitamehta.com
Website: www.nitamehta.com

Editorial and Marketing office
E-159, Greater Kailash II, New Delhi 110 048

Food Styling and Photography by Snab
Typesetting by National Information Technology Academy
3A/3, Asaf Ali Road, New Delhi 110 002

Recipe Development & Testing:
Nita Mehta Foods - R & D Centre
3A/3, Asaf Ali Road, New Delhi - 110002

ISBN 978-81-7869-321-7

First Edition 2013

Cover Designed by: flyingtrees

Distributed by :
NITA MEHTA BOOKS
3A/3, Asaf Ali Road, New Delhi - 02
Distribution Centre :
D16/1, Okhla Industrial Area, Phase-I,
New Delhi - 110020
Tel.: 26813199, 26813200
E-mail: nitamehta.mehta@gmail.com

Contributing Writers :
Anurag Mehta
Tanya Mehta
Subhash Mehta
Editors :
Sangeeta
Sunita

Printed in India at Infinity Advertising Services (P) Ltd, New Delhi

Price: Rs. 595/- US$ 24.95 UK£ 19.95

Introduction

India has every kind of climate zone within its borders: extremely wet areas drenched with monsoon rain; dry sandy deserts; fertile river-watered plains; balmy hills and valleys; snow-covered mountains; and a very long coastline.

Each climate zone has its own flora and fauna, the 'raw material' for the region's food, at the basic level. But apart from a varied climate, there is also tremendous diversity in history, culture and tradition, which gets superimposed on the preparation of food, and refines it to a sophisticated art. So in every part of India – a region, a state, a city – you will find a distinct cuisine that has evolved over centuries, with recipes perfected and passed down from generation to generation.

Come, let us take a Taste Exploration Journey around India together.

Nita Mehta

taste of...

Kashmir 17

Kashmiri Kahwa 18
Nadru Yakhni 20
Roghan Josh 22
Dum Aloo 24
Gushtaba 26

Punjab 29

Amritsari Machhi 30
Paneer Tikka 32
Chicken Malai Tikka 34
Dahi Pudina Chutney 34
Dal Makhani (Maanh Sabut) 36
Tandoori Chicken 38
Sarson ka Saag 40
Makki ki Roti 40

Delhi 43

Aloo ki Tikki 44
Gole Gappe 46
Butter Chicken 48
Paneer Kathi Rolls 50
Kadhai Paneer 52

Rajasthan 55

Khoye wale Shahi Gatte ... 56
Dal-Bati-Churma 58
Laal Maans 60
Bajra Roti aur Lahsuni Chutney 62
Bajre ki Khichri 62

Lucknow 65

Kachori aur Chatpati Aloo Bhaji 66
Avadh ke Shahi Kofte 68
Galouti Kebab 70
Lucknow ki Khaas Degh-e-Biryani 72
Jalebi 74

Gujarat 77

Khakra 78
Methi Thepla 78
Chundo 78
Khandvi 80
Instant Khaman Dhokla 82
Undhiyu 84
Shrikhand 86
Aam Ras 86

...the authentic and traditional way !

taste of...

Bengal 89

Ghugni 90
Masala Jhinga 90
Bengali Machcher Jhol 92
Shukto 94
Kesari Sandesh 96
Rasgulla 98

Mumbai 101

Chowpatty ki Bhel 102
Mumbai ka Kala Khatta 102
Ragda Pattise 104
Misal Pav 106
Falooda 108

Goa 111

Spicy Goan Crab Soup 112
Fish Curry 114
Goanese Chicken 116
Prawn Vindaloo 118
Mushroom Xacuti 120

Hyderabad 123

Parda Subz Biryani 124
Mirch ka Salan 126
Tamatar Kut 128
Haleem 130
Mutton-Bhindi ka Shorva 132
Sheermal 134
Khubani ka Mitha 134

Tamil Nadu 137

Kurma Kuzhambu 138
Chicken Chettinad 140
Tomato Chutney 140
Tamarind Rice 142

Karnataka 145

Masala Poori 146
Kori Sukkha 146
Kori Gassi 148
Bisi Bele Bhath 150

Kerala 153

Appam with Vegetable Stew 154
Avial 156
Thoran 156
Karimeen 158
Malabar Parotha 158

International Conversion Guide 160
Glossary of Herbs & Spices 161
Glossary of Regional Cuisines of India 162

...the authentic and traditional way !

The seeding...

The cycle of Nature brings fertile water to the land. A seed is planted and it grows and grows. It feeds the cattle and it feeds the man. They work together to plant more seeds to create abundance . . .

The outburst...

The sun shines bright and hot on tender shoots and leaves of palest green. Roots dig deep into the earth and drink the water greedily. Above the earth, the sap rises, the stem stretches, and the leaves unfurl. The field sways in an outburst of exhilaration . . .

The harvesting...

Steeped in the warmth of the days, lulled through cool nights, the harvest is ready, richly golden, offering health, wealth and happiness. The harvest must be cut and baled and carried away for safe storage. There is grain in every household for the coming months. The people rejoice and give thanks . . .

The packing...

A long journey to feed the hungry in the towns. Sacks are stitched and weighed, stacked on ships and trains and trucks. From this patch of farm land, to your table . . .

The celebrations...

It was worth waiting for the water to flow, the sun to pour its heat, the seeds to grow, the harvest to ripen . . . . . The village rings with harvest songs of celebration. The dancing steps keep to the rhythm of the beating heart. The future is ours!

The diversity...

From the bountiful ocean, fish are caught in nets of ingenious design. A harvest from the sea, so good to eat, such a generous gift of Nature . . .

The good-bye...

The farmer says good bye . . . . . he has sold his carefully nurtured product and sent it off to unknown places, unknown people.

You go to the market with your shopping bag and look at the wonderful colours and textures of the fruit and vegetables, grains and spices, gathered there in one place. You fill your bag and hurry home to cook a meal for your loved ones . . .

कृपा
अक्षया
PLEASE
आशिर्वाद

AIRCEL

taste of Kashmir

In Kashmir, a carpet of spring flowers spreads over the mountainside as fast as the snow melts away. Fields of purple crocus bear saffron stamens which have to be delicately plucked out by hand and dried. Saffron gives its aroma to the famous hot drink called kahwa, made with green tea.

Streams and lakes provide plenty of fish. Lotus plants thrive on the lakes and their roots, nadru, are used to make traditional delicacies.

Over the centuries, migrants came from Central Asia – wood carvers and weavers and also cooks called waza. The traditional banquet is called wazwan, a formal meal, almost a ceremony, to offer hospitality to guests. Dish after dish is served, each carefully prepared with fragrant herbs and choicest ingredients. Delicacies such as Methi and Tabakmaaz, Roganjosh and Rista and a variety of kababs and vegetable dishes are served. The meal continues with Goashtaba, followed by a dessert such as Phirni, and finally a cup of kahwa.

Fennel, dried ginger, mild Kashmiri red chillies, cinnamon and cardamom are the typical spices that flavour the food. Yogurt and cream are used generously. Walnuts, almonds and pine nuts, and all kinds of fruit, are grown locally and enrich the cuisine.

Boats in the famous Dal Lake of Kashmir.

Kashmiri Kahwa

A saffron-scented green tea from Kashmir enriched with almonds.

Makes 2 cups

INGREDIENTS

- 2¼ cups water
- 1 tsp green tea leaves
- 2 tsp sugar, or to taste
- 2 green cardamoms (*chhoti elaichi*) - powdered
- 2 pinches of cinnamon (*dalchini)* powder
- 4-6 strands of saffron (*kesar*)

TOPPING

- 3-4 almonds (*badam*) - slivered (cut into thin long pieces)

METHOD

1. Mix all the ingredients in a saucepan. Boil. Simmer for 5 minutes.
2. Strain tea into the cups.
3. Top each cup with some slivered almonds. Serve hot.

Note: Kahwa is good for digestion. You can omit sugar if desired.

Nadru Yakhni

Lotus stem is called Nadru in Kashmir and is considered a delicacy.

Serves 4-5

INGREDIENTS

- 400 gms lotus stem (*nadru*)
- 4 tbsp oil
- a pinch asafoetida (*hing*)
- 4 cloves (*laung*)
- 6-7 peppercorns (*sabut kali mirch*)
- 1" cinnamon (*dalchini*)
- 1 black cardamom (*moti elaichi*)
- 3 cardamoms (*chhoti elaichi*) - pounded
- 1 bay leaf (*tej patta*)
- ½ tsp salt

MIX TOGETHER

- 1½ cups fresh yogurt (*well beaten*)
- 1 tsp crushed fennel seeds (*saunf*)
- crushed seeds of 1 black cardamom
- 1" cinnamon stick - crushed
- ½ tsp royal cumin - crushed
- ½ tsp salt
- 1 tsp coriander powder
- 1 tsp dry ginger powder (*sonth*)

TEMPERING

- 1-2 tbsp *ghee*
- 1 tsp royal cumin (*shah jeera*)
- 2 dry red chillies

METHOD

1. Peel lotus stem. Wash a cut diagonally into ¼" to ½" thick pieces. Clean the dirt if any with a tooth pick.
2. Put in a pressure cook with ½ cup water. Add ½ tsp salt, asafoetida, cloves, peppercorns, cinnamon, bay leaf, cardamoms and black cardamom. Allow one whistle. Remove from heat and let it cool down.
3. In a *kadhai* heat 4 tbsp oil. Add cut lotus stems. Sauté for 4-5 minutes. Keep aside.
4. Whisk yogurt till smooth. Crush spices - fennel, seeds of black cardamom, cinnamon and royal cumin. Add these spices to the whisked yogurt. Also add salt, coriander powder and dry ginger powder to the yogurt.
5. Warm 2 tbsp oil in a pan on low heat. Add the yogurt mix and stir continuously on very low heat for 3-4 minutes till slightly thick.
6. Add the sautéd lotus stem slices. Stir for 3-4 minutes till done and some gravy remains. Remove from heat.
7. Heat 1 tbsp *ghee*. Reduce heat. Add royal cumin and dry red chillies. When the cumin turns golden, pour the *ghee* on top of the cooked lotus stem. Mix well and serve.

Roghan Josh

The very popular mutton curry.

Serves 2-3

INGREDIENTS

- 250 gms mutton
- 3 tbsp *ghee*/oil
- 2 cloves (*laung*)
- ½" cinnamon (*dalchini*)
- 1 black cardamom (*moti elaichi*)
- 1 bay leaf (*tej patta*)
- ¼ tsp asafoetida (*hing*) dissolved in 1 tsp water
- ¾ tsp fennel powder (*saunf*)
- ¼ tsp dry ginger powder (*sonth*)
- ½ tsp ginger paste
- 1 tsp red chilli powder (*degi mirch*)
- ¾ tsp salt, or to taste
- ¼ tsp pepper powder
- 8 tbsp yogurt (*optional*)
- 4 green cardamoms (*chhoti elaichi*) - powdered
- a little saffron (*kesar*) - dissolved in warm water

METHOD

1. Heat *ghee*/oil in a pressure cooker. Add cloves, cinnamon, black cardamom and bay leaf. Fry for 1 minute.
2. Add mutton and asafoetida water. Fry for 4-5 minutes till well fried. The mutton should become brownish in colour.
3. Add fennel, dry ginger powder, ginger paste, red chilli powder, salt and pepper. Stir for 3-4 minutes.
4. Reduce heat. Add powdered cardamoms and yogurt. Keep stirring till it boils.
5. Add ½ cup water. Close the cooker and give 4-5 whistles. (Mutton should become tender)
6. Open the cooker after the pressure drops. Add saffron. Simmer for 2-3 minutes and serve.

Note: *Some people do not like to add yogurt as the yogurt beats the colour. Then add 1 cup water and omit curd.*

Some people add little water in which ratanjot has been dissolved (to give a fiery red colour). Amount of gravy is an individual choice. Some people keep little gravy where as others fry it to such an extent that only oil remains. The cooking time will depend upon the quality of mutton.

Dum Aloo

This dish is a medley of aromatic spices blended in a spicy gravy with fried potatoes.

Serves 4-5 cups

INGREDIENTS

- 400 gms (8-9) medium potatoes
- 4 tbsp oil
- 4 cloves (*laung*)
- 1" cinnamon (*dalchini*)
- 1 bay leaf (*tej patta*)
- ¼ tsp asafoetida (*hing*) dissolved in 1 tsp water
- 1 tsp dry ginger powder (*sonth*)
- 2 tsp fennel powder (*saunf*)
- 1½-2 tsp red chilli powder (*degi mirch*)
- 1 tsp salt
- 1 black cardamom (*moti elaichi*) - coarsely powdered
- oil for frying

METHOD

1. To boil potatoes, put them in a pressure cooker with about 3 cups water. Pressure cook to give 1 whistle. Remove from heat and put under running water to release pressure. Cool the potatoes.
2. Peel and prick the cooled potatoes all over with a tooth pick.
3. Heat oil and deep fry potatoes all together, to a rich golden brown colour.
4. Heat 4 tbsp oil. Add cloves, bay leaf and cinnamon. Fry for 1 minute.
5. Add asafoetida water. Cook for ½ minute. Add red chilli powder. Fry for ½ minute. Add 1 cup water.
6. Add all other ingredients and the fried potatoes.
7. Cover and simmer till very little gravy remains and oil floats on top.
8. Break one potato and see. The inside should not be white. The colour of the chillies should have penetrated to the centre of the potatoes. If the potato is white from inside add a little more water and simmer for some more time.
9. Serve hot with boiled rice.

Delicious large sized koftas in yogurt gravy. The addition of dried mint is important as it gives a deliciously different taste to the dish.

Serves 4

INGREDIENTS - KOFTA (mix together)

- 250 gms mutton mince (*keema*), chicken mince can also be used
- 1 tsp fennel power (*saunf*)
- ½ tsp dry ginger powder (*sonth*)
- ¾ tsp salt
- ½ tsp cumin powder (*jeera*)
- seeds of 1 black cardamom (*moti elaichi*) - powdered

TO BOIL KOFTAS

- 1½ cups water
- 1" cinnamon (*dalchini*)
- 1 bay leaf (*tej patta*)
- 2-3 cloves (*laung*)
- ½ tsp salt

GRAVY

- 2 tbsp oil
- 2 tbsp *ghee*
- 1 medium onion - sliced
- 1 cup yogurt - beaten well
- ½ tsp fennel powder (*saunf*)
- ¼ tsp dry ginger powder (*sonth*)
- ¼ tsp *garam masala*
- ½-1 tsp dried mint (*pudina*)
- seeds of 1 big cardamom (*moti elaichi*) powdered
- 2 green cardamoms (*chhoti elaichi*) - powdered

METHOD

1. Grind mince in the mixer to a fine paste.
2. Mix all ingredients under koftas well together. Shape into 4 large balls.
3. Heat 2-3 cups water in a small pan with salt, cinnamon, bay leaf and cloves. When it boils add the koftas. Cook covered on medium heat for about 20 minutes or till tender/cooked. Overturn in between to cook all sides. If using chicken mince, cook only for 7-8 minutes.
4. Heat oil in a *kadhai*. Add *ghee* and sliced onion. Fry till golden brown. Remove from heat. Remove onions from oil. Cook and grind to a fine paste with a little water. Keep brown onion paste aside.
5. In the same oil add well beaten yogurt, fennel, dry ginger powder, *garam masala*, mint and cardamom powder. Keep on low heat. Stir till it boils.
6. Add onion paste. Mix well for a minute.
7. Add cooked koftas/*gushtabas* along with any water that is remaining after boiling the koftas. Cover and simmer for 15-20 minutes.
8. Serve garnished with fresh mint leaves.

taste of Punjab

Punjab lies in a fertile plain criss-crossed by rivers and irrigation canals. It is the prosperous bread basket of India. Milk and its products in the form of malai (cream), paneer (cottage cheese), butter, ghee, yogurt, and buttermilk are an important part of every meal.

The main masala base for curries is made from onions, garlic, ginger and tomatoes sautéed in pure ghee. Chicken is favoured by non-vegetarians, as much as paneer is favoured by vegetarians. Mah ki Dal, Sarson Ka Saag, Makki ki Roti, hearty meat curries and paranthas stuffed with a variety of fillings can be found in no other state except Punjab.

The people are energetic and hard working, and know how to enjoy life to the fullest. The colour and vibrancy of their culture can be seen in the folk songs and dances such as the bhangra.

The cuisine of this robust agricultural community mirrors their attitude – healthy local products that give energy to work on the farm. Ghee or mustard oil is the cooking medium. Homemade white butter is lavishly spread on bread made of wheat or maize flour. Black lentils and kidney beans become creamy with slow cooking. A tandoor (clay oven) bakes fish, chicken, mutton or naan bread to perfection, adding its own smoky flavour.

In this wheat-dominated cuisine, rice is cooked to pair it with rajma and karhi. In a unique dessert, called Rao ki Kheer, rice is simmered in sugarcane juice for hours together on a slow fire.

The Sunflower fields of Punjab.

Amritsari Machhi

Delicious fried fish with the flavour of carom seeds. Makes an excellent snack.

Serves 5-6

INGREDIENTS

- 800 gms fish (18-20 pieces), preferably boneless and generally Sole fish is used but any fish can be used
- 2 tbsp plus 8 tbsp gram flour (*besan*)
- some *chaat masala* for sprinkling on top
- oil for frying

MARINADE

- 1 tsp carom seeds (*ajwain*)
- 3 tsp garlic paste
- 3 tsp ginger paste
- 2 tsp salt
- 2 tsp red chilli powder
- 1½ tsp *garam masala*
- 8-10 tbsp lemon juice

METHOD

1. Rub fish with 1 tsp salt and 2 tbsp gram flour. Wash well to remove all smell.
2. Mix together all ingredients of the marinade.
3. Rub this marinade on the fish and leave the fish to marinate for 2-3 hours in the fridge.
4. At the time of serving, sprinkle 8 tbsp gram flour on fish and rub it so that the gram flour lightly coats the fish. Sprinkle more gram flour if needed.
5. Deep fry to a golden brown colour till the fish is cooked and crisp.
6. Sprinkle *chaat masala* and serve hot garnished with onion rings, lemon wedges and sprigs of coriander or mint.

Note:

1. *A few drops of colour (orange red) can be added to the marinade for a different colour.*
2. *For a different flavour 1-1½ tsp dry fenugreek leaves (kasuri methi) can be added in the marinade.*

Paneer Tikka

Freshly grilled cottage cheese cubes marinated in spices and yoghurt taste awesome.

Serves 4

INGREDIENTS

- 400 gms paneer - cut into 1½" piece
- 1 capsicum - cut into 1" pieces
- 1 large onion - cut into 8 pieces
- 4 tbsp gram flour (*besan*) - roasted
- 4-5 tbsp thick cream or fresh *malai*
- ¾ cup yogurt - hang in a muslin cloth for 30 minutes
- 1 tsp salt
- ½ tsp red chilli powder
- ½ tsp *garam masala*
- a few drops orange red food colour
- 3-4 tbsp chopped mint (*pudina*) leaves
- few toothpicks (optional)

GRIND TOGETHER TO A PASTE

- 1" piece ginger
- 6-8 flakes garlic
- 1 tsp cumin seeds (*jeera*)
- seeds of 2 green cardamoms (*chhoti elaichi*)
- 2 tbsp chopped fresh coriander
- 2-3 green chillies
- 2 tbsp cashewnuts (*kaju)*

METHOD

1. Grind ginger, garlic, cumin seeds, green cardamoms, coriander, green chillies and cashewnuts to a paste.
2. Add roasted gram flour, cream, hung yogurt, salt, chilli powder and garam masala to the paste. Add enough orange red food colour to the paste to get a nice colour. Add mint leaves.
3. Cut *paneer* into 1½" cubes. Put the paste in a big bowl and add the *paneer* pieces and mix well so as to coat the paste nicely on all the pieces. Add the onion and capsicum pieces also and mix. Keep aside for 1 hour in the refrigerator or till serving time.
4. Pre-heat the oven or tandoor on moderate flame.
5. Cover the wire rack of the oven with foil and grease well. Place the marinated *paneer* pieces and vegetables on it. Rub the left over marinade on the pieces.
6. Grill for about 10 minutes in the pre-heated oven till golden. Baste with melted butter or oil in between. Serve as it is or skewer on toothpicks.

Chicken Malai Tikka

Tender, melt in the mouth kebabs of boneless chicken flavoured with herbs and grilled.

Serves 4-6

INGREDIENTS

- 500 gms boneless chicken - cut into 1" pieces

FIRST MARINADE

- 2 tbsp white vinegar
- 1 tsp salt, ½ tsp white pepper powder
- 1 tsp ginger paste, 1 tbsp garlic paste
- 2 tbsp oil

SECOND MARINADE

- 1½ cups yogurt - hang in a muslin cloth for 1 hour
- 3 tbsp broken cashewnuts - soak in ¼ cup hot water for 1 hour and then grind to a smooth paste in a mixer
- ¼ cup grated cheddar cheese
- 3 tbsp oil, 1 egg white
- 2 tbsp chopped green coriander
- 1 tbsp finely chopped green chillies
- 3-4 tbsp cream, 1 tsp butter
- ½ tsp black salt, ½ tsp salt
- ¼ tsp white pepper powder
- 2 tbsp lemon juice
- ½ tsp mace powder (*javitri*)
- ¼ tsp green cardamom (*elaichi*) powder
- 1 tsp tandoori masala

METHOD

1. Wash the chicken pieces and pat dry on a kitchen towel. Marinate the pieces in the first marinade for 1 hour in the fridge.
2. In a flat dish place cheese. Rub with the palms till smooth. Add hung yogurt, mix thoroughly until cheese is smoothly mixed with the yogurt. Add egg white and mix well. Add the remaining ingredients of second marinade. Mix till smooth.
3. Add the marinated chicken pieces. Mix. Keep in refrigerator till serving time.
4. Cover the wire rack of the oven with a well greased foil. Place the marinated chicken pieces on it. Rub the left over marinade on the pieces.
5. Cook for 15-20 minutes in the *pre-heat*ed oven at 180°C till well-browned and cooked (if the chicken is not well browned from top after getting cooked from inside then put the chicken in the grill mode for 2-3 minutes). Serve hot with green *chutney*.

Dahi Pudina Chutney

INGREDIENTS - GRIND TOGETHER

- ½ cup mint (*pudina*)
- 1 cup fresh coriander
- 2 green chillies, ½ onion
- 2 flakes garlic

ADD LATER

- ½ cup yogurt - hang for 15 minutes
- 1 tsp oil, 1 tsp lemon juice
- a pinch of rock salt (*kala namak*)
- ¼ tsp roasted cumin (*bhuna jeera*)

METHOD

1. Grind coriander, mint, green chillies, onion and garlic with a little water to a paste. Beat hung yogurt and add to the green paste. Add remaining ingredients also.

Dal Makhani (Maanh Sabut)

A well blended and creamy preparation of black lentils.

Serves 6

INGREDIENTS

- 1 cup black lentils (*urad sabut dal*)
- 2 tbsp split gram *dal* (*channe ki dal*)
- 2 tbsp kidney beans (*rajmah*), optional - soaked for at least 6 hours or overnight
- 1 tbsp *ghee* or oil
- 5 cups of water
- 1½ tsp salt
- 2 dry whole red chillies, preferably *Kashmiri* red chillies
- 1" piece ginger
- 4 flakes garlic (optional)
- 4 tomatoes - pureed in a grinder
- 1 tbsp dry fenugreek leaves (*kasuri methi*)
- 3 tbsp *ghee* or oil
- 2 tsp coriander powder (*dhania*)
- ½ tsp *garam masala*
- 2 tbsp butter
- ¼ cup fresh *malai,* beaten well and mixed with ¼ cup milk to make it ½ cup or ½ cup cream

METHOD

1. Clean, wash *dals.* If you want to add kidney beans, soak both *dals* and kidney beans together in a pressure cooker for 6 hours or overnight.
2. Grind ginger and garlic together to a paste.
3. Discard water from the soaked *dals* and add 5 cups of fresh water.
4. Pressure cook both *dals* and kidney beans with 1 tbsp *ghee*, salt, half of the ginger-garlic paste and the dry, red chillies. Keep the left over paste aside.
5. After the first whistle, keep on low flame for 40 minutes. Remove from fire. After the pressure drops, mash the hot *dal* a little. Keep aside.
6. Heat *ghee.* Add tomatoes pureed in a grinder. Cook until thick and dry.
7. Add the left over ginger-garlic paste, *garam masala* and coriander powder. Cook until *ghee* separates.
8. Add dry fenugreek leaves. Cook further for 1-2 minutes.
9. Add this tomato mixture to the boiled *dal.*
10. Add butter. Simmer on low flame for 20-25 minutes, stirring and mashing the *dal* occasionally with a *kadchhi* against the sides of the cooker.
11. Add beaten *malai* mixed with milk or cream. Mix very well with a *kadchhi.* Simmer for 15-20 minutes more, to get the right colour and smoothness. Remove from heat. Serve hot.

Note: *Originally the dal was cooked by leaving it overnight on the burning coal angithis. The longer the dal simmered, the better it tasted.*

Tandoori Chicken

An all time favourite of not only Punjabis but all people fond of good food.

Serves 4-5

INGREDIENTS

- 1 chicken (1 kg) - cut into 8 pieces
- 6 tbsp yogurt
- 2 tbsp plain flour (*maida*)
- a pinch of orange red food colour
- 1 small onion - grated (2 tbsp)
- 1 tsp garlic paste
- 1 tsp ginger paste
- 1 tbsp dry fenugreek leaves (*kasoori methi*)
- 1½ tsp salt
- ½ tsp cumin powder (*jeera*)
- ½ tsp coriander powder (*dhania*)
- 1 tsp red chilli powder
- ½ tsp *garam masala* powder
- 1½ tsp chicken tandoori masala

METHOD

1. Mix yogurt, plain flour, colour and all other ingredients. Add enough colour to get a bright orange colour.
2. Wash chicken. Squeeze out all excess water. Pat dry on a clean kitchen towel.
3. Marinate chicken in the yogurt mixture for 2-3 hours in the refrigerator.
4. Rub the wire rack of the oven with oil and place the marinated chicken on it, so that the extra marinade can drip down from the grill. If the chicken is placed in a tray, the extra marinade and liquid keep collecting around the chicken pieces and hence they do not turn dry and crisp.
5. Roast for 8-10 minutes in an oven at 180°C.
6. Overturn again, brush with oil and cook for another 10-12 minutes or till tender and crisp. Serve hot garnished with onion rings and lemon wedges.

Note:

1. *Instead of a full chicken only drumsticks (legs) can be made. They are called tangdi kebabs. After grilling, wrap a piece of aluminium foil at the end of each leg. Besides looking nice, it is also convenient for holding and eating the chicken leg.*
2. *Boneless chicken cut into 1½"-2" pieces can be cooked in a similar manner to get chicken tikka.*
3. *Tandoori chicken can be added to an onion-tomato masala for a tikka masala dish.*
4. *For chicken tikka, in the marinade instead of plain flour, gram flour can be added for a different flavour.*
5. *Fish tikka is also made this way. Use boneless and skinless 2"-3" pieces of fish.*

Sarson ka Saag

Mustard greens tempered with clarified butter and served with maize flour bread is a favourite in Punjab.

Serves 6

INGREDIENTS

- 1 bundle (1 kg) mustard greens (*sarson*)
- 250 gms spinach or *baathoo*
- 2 turnips (*shalgam*) - peeled and chopped, optional
- 3-4 flakes garlic - finely chopped
- 2" piece ginger - finely chopped
- 1 green chilli - chopped
- ¾ tsp salt, or to taste
- 2 tbsp maize flour (*makki ka atta*)
- 1½ tsp powdered jaggery (*gur*)

TADKA/TEMPERING

- 3 tbsp *ghee*
- 2 green chillies - finely chopped
- 1" piece ginger - finely chopped
- ½ tsp red chilli powder

METHOD

1. Wash and clean mustard leaves. First remove the leaves and then peel the stems, starting from the lower end and chop them finely. (Peel stems the way you string green beans). The addition of stems to the *saag* makes it tastier but it is important to peel the stems from the lower ends. The upper tender portion may just be chopped. Chop the spinach or *baathoo* leaves and mix with mustard greens.
2. Put chopped greens with ½ cup water in a deep pan.
3. Chop garlic, ginger and green chilli very finely and add to the greens, add turnips if you wish. Add salt and put it on fire and let it start heating. The greens will start going down. Cover and let it cook on medium heat for 15-20 minutes. Remove from heat, cool.
4. Grind to a coarse paste. Do not grind too much.
5. Add maize flour to the greens and cook for 15 minutes on low heat.
6. At serving time, heat *ghee*. Reduce heat and add ginger and green chillies. Cook till ginger changes colour. Remove from heat and add red chilli powder. Add *ghee* to the hot *saag* and mix lightly. Serve with fresh home-made butter and *makki-ki-roti*.

Makki ki Roti

Makes 6-7

INGREDIENTS

- 2 cups maize flour (*makki ka atta*)
- ¼ tsp salt
- hot water to knead the flour
- *ghee* or oil to fry the *roti*

METHOD

1. Sieve the flour with salt. Just before making the *rotis,* knead the flour with hot water to a smooth dough. Do not knead the dough too much in advance.
2. Tear a plastic bag into two halves. Keep one piece on the rolling platform (*chakla*). Put 1 ball of the kneaded dough on the plastic. Cover with the other piece, such that there is a plastic cover above and beneath the ball. Roll carefully to a slightly thick *roti.*
3. Cook *roti* on a hot griddle on both sides, and fry on low flame with 1-2 tsp ghee.

नमकीन काजू • बादाम रोगन • केशर • आलू बुखारा • गुच्छी • डिगरी
380
400
360
320
400
360
200
160
360
140
320

taste of Delhi

Delhi is a joy for food lovers as every kind of cuisine is available here, reflecting its journey through the historical chain of events from the past, or from recent history, to the present. But what is uniquely 'Delhi' is the excellence of its Dhaba Food and Street Food – the original Fast Food pioneers.

Dhabas are low cost eateries serving hearty and tasty fare. One item that appears on all dhaba menus is Butter Chicken – though this dish was supposedly 'invented' in a restaurant called Moti Mahal in Daryagunj, on the edge of the Old City. It became a big hit and has now found a place on every Indian menu worldwide.

The epicentre of Street Food in the Old City, in Chandini Chowk where you will find rows of chaat wallas, halwais, namkeen walas and even a street named paranthey wali gali.

The chaat has just the right balance of hot-spicy and tangy-sweet. Papdi Chaat, with Kachalu Chutney and Khasta Puri, liberally doused with saunth, the chutney made with jaggery, tamarind and dried ginger. Aloo Tikki, Dahi Bhalla, and Fruit Chaat are also there to tempt you. A hot meal of Channa Masala with Bhature will not make a hole in your pocket but fill your stomach well. All kinds of Kathi Rolls are the newest way to have a meal-on-the go.

Nuts and spice market in Delhi.

Aloo ki Tikki

Pan fried potato tikki with a delicious lentil filling.

Makes 8

INGREDIENTS

- 6 big potatoes - boiled and mashed
- 5 tbsp *arrowroot* or cornflour
- 1 tsp salt
- ½ tsp red chilli powder
- 2 white bread slices
- 5-6 tbsp *ghee* or oil for shallow frying

FILLING

- ½ cup split, yellow moong beans (*dhuli moong dal*) - soak for 1-2 hours in warm water
- ½ tsp cumin seeds (*jeera*)
- 2 pinches asafoetida (*hing*)
- 2 tsp finely chopped ginger
- 2 green chillies - finely chopped
- ½ tsp salt, ¼ tsp turmeric powder
- 1 tsp coriander powder
- ¾ tsp red chilli powder
- ¾ tsp *garam masala*
- 1 tbsp gram flour (*besan*)
- 1 tbsp coriander leaves - chopped
- ½ tsp chat *masala* or to taste

METHOD

1. For the filling, drain *dal* and keep aside. Heat 3 tbsp oil or *ghee* in a *kadhai.* Add cumin and asafoetida. Let cumin turn golden. Remove from heat. Add ginger, chopped green chillies and stir. Add all dry *masala*s - salt, turmeric, coriander powder, red chilli powder and *garam masala*. Return to heat. Add *dal.* Stir for about 2 minutes on low medium heat. Add ½ cup water and cook covered for 7-8 minutes till soft. Uncover and dry water if any. Add gram flour and stir for 2-3 minutes. Add coriander and chat *masala* to taste and saute for 2-3 minutes. Remove from heat and keep aside to cool.
2. Boil, peel and grate potatoes. Sprinkle *arrowroot*/cornflour, 1 tsp salt and red chilli powder on potatoes. Dip a slice in water for a second and squeeze completely. Add to the potatoes. Repeat with the second slice. Mix well. Check seasonings.
3. Divide the potato mixture into 8 portions. Take a ball of mashed potatoes on your greased palm. Make a shallow cup with the ball of mashed potatoes by pressing in the centre. Place a tbsp full of *dal* filling in centre and seal well from all sides to cover the filling.
4. Heat oil on a griddle (*tawa*) for shallow frying. Put 3 tikkis at a time on medium heat till golden and crisp on both sides. Once done, shift to the sides and put fresh ones in the centre till really crisp. Serve hot.

FREE HOME DELIVERY IN SOUTH DELHI
ANUP

Gol Gappe

Round hollow crispy balls which are filled with spicy water.

Serves 4

INGREDIENTS

- ½ cup semolina (*suji*)
- ½ cup whole wheat flour (*atta*)
- ½ tsp salt
- 1/3 cup soda water (a bottle of soda)

METHOD

1. Mix semolina, whole wheat flour and salt. Knead to a stiff dough with soda water. Cover dough with wet muslin cloth *(mal-mal ka kapda)* and keep aside for 20 minutes.
2. Divide dough into 2 balls. On a floured surface, roll out a ball thinly and evenly. Cut into small rounds with a sharp lid of a bottle or a cookie cutter.
3. Spread a wet cotton cloth and keep *puris* on it and cover with another wet cloth.
4. Roll trimmings again and re use.
5. Heat oil in a *kadhai.* Put one *puri* in oil and press lightly with a pauni till it puffs. Turn and then quickly slide the second one in oil. Keep putting the next in oil when the one already in oil has bean turned. Fry 4-5 this way. Once all are in, turn the *puris* and fry on low heat till golden brown. Keep the dough covered. Store *puris* in an air tight container.

FILLING

- ½ cup chick peas (*kabuli channe*) or dry peas - soaked overnight
- 1 large potato - boiled & chopped
- ½ tsp roasted cumin (*bhuna jeera*)
- ¼ tsp dry mango powder (*amchoor*)
- ¼ tsp black salt
- ¼ tsp red chilli powder, or to taste
- some tamarind (*imli*) *chutney*

METHOD

1. Pressure cook chickpeas or dry peas with ½ cup water, ½ tsp salt and a pinch soda to a whistle. Reduce heat and cook for 10 minutes. Let the pressure drop. Strain. Add boiled potato, salt and spices. Mix well.

TAMARIND WATER

- ¾ cup chopped fresh coriander leaves
- 1-2 green chillies
- 2 lemon sized ball of tamarind - soaked in 1 cup water
- a pinch of asafoetida (*hing*)
- 2 tsp black salt
- ½ tsp salt
- 2-3 tsp roasted cumin (*bhuna jeera*)
- 3 cups water, 2-3 tbsp *boondi*

METHOD

1. Grind coriander and green chillies to a fine paste. Add water and all the remaining ingredients. Check salt and seasonings. Chill.

FREE HOME DELIVERY IN SOUTH DELHI
ANUP

Butter Chicken

Chicken cooked in a fragrant red coloured sauce made in butter.

Serves 4

INGREDIENTS

- 1 medium sized chicken (800 gms) - cut into 12 pieces
- ½ cup yogurt - hang for 45 minutes in a muslin cloth
- 1 tbsp garlic paste
- 1 tbsp dry fenugreek leaves (*kasuri methi*)
- ½ tsp rock salt (*kala namak),* 1 tsp *garam masala,* ½ tsp salt

GRAVY

Boil Together

- ½ kg (6-7) tomatoes - roughly chopped
- ½" piece ginger
- 10 flakes garlic - finely chopped
- 2 green chillies - chopped
- 5-6 cloves (*laung*)
- 4-5 green cardamoms (*chhoti elaichi*) - pounded to open
- 1½ tsp *degi mirch*
- 2 cups water

Other Ingredients

- 4 tbsp oil
- 2 tsp ginger-garlic paste
- 1 tsp *kashmiri* red chilli pd (*degi mirch*)
- 2 tbsp butter, ¼ cup cream
- 4 tbsp cashewnuts (*kaju*) - soak in ¼ cup hot water for 15 minutes, grind to a smooth paste
- ½ tsp *garam masala*
- 1 tsp salt, or to taste
- 2 tsp *tandoori masala* (optional)
- ¼ tsp sugar or to taste
- 1 tbsp dry fenugreek leaves (*kasuri methi*) - dry roasted on a griddle for 2 minutes and crushed to a powder
- pinch of orange food colour

METHOD

1. Wash and pat dry chicken. For the marinade, mix hung yogurt, garlic paste, dry fenugreek leaves, black salt, *garam masala* and colour. Rub the chicken with this mixture. Keep aside for 30 mins or preferably overnight in the refrigerator.
2. Heat 6 tbsp oil in a *kadhai*, add marinated chicken, cook on high heat for 5-6 minutes, stirring all the time. Reduce heat and cook covered for about 10 minutes or till tender. Remove from heat. Keep aside.
3. To prepare the *makhani* gravy, boil tomatoes with all the ingredients. Reduce heat and cook covered on low heat for 15 minutes till slightly reduced in quantity. Remove from heat. Cool completely for 15 minutes. Grind to a smooth puree. Strain puree through a metal strainer.
4. Heat 4 tbsp oil in a *kadhai.* Add 2 tsp ginger-garlic paste and stir till golden. Add 1 tsp *degi mirch.* Stir and add prepared tomato puree. Boil. Cook for 5-7 minutes. Add all the remaining ingredients of the gravy. Bring to a boil, stirring continuously. Cook on medium heat till you get the desired colour and thickness of the gravy. Add a pinch of colour if needed. Add cooked chicken. Simmer for 2 minutes till the gravy turns to a bright colour. Garnish with 1 tbsp of fresh cream and slit green chillies. Serve hot.

FREE HOME DELIVERY IN SOUTH DELHI

Paneer Kathi Rolls

Wraps of fresh cottage cheese flavoured with mint and coriander.

Makes 8

- 8 Roomali Rotis or flour tortillas

FILLING

- 300 gms *paneer* - cut into thin fingers
- 2 tbsp oil
- ½ tsp cumin seeds (*jeera*)
- ¼ tsp onion seeds (*kalaunji*)
- ¼ tsp fennel (*saunf*)
- 2 green chillies - chopped
- 4 onions - cut into thin slices
- 1½ cups shredded cabbage
- 2 capsicums - cut into thin strips
- ½ tsp turmeric (*haldi*)
- ½ tsp dry mango powder (*amchoor*)
- ¾ cup chopped fresh coriander
- 4 tbsp mint - chopped roughly or torn with hands
- 4 tbsp tomato ketchup
- 1½ tsp salt
- ¼ tsp pepper powder
- ¾ tsp garam masala
- ½ tsp red chilli powder
- 1 tsp chaat masala
- 1 tomato - de-seeded & cut into 1" long thin fingers

TO SPREAD

- 4-5 tbsp green chutney mixed with 1-2 tsp tomato ketchup

METHOD

1. For making the filling of *kathi* roll, heat 2 tbsp oil in a pan. Add cumin, onion seeds and fennel. Wait till cumin turns golden.
2. Add green chillies, stir.
3. Add onions and stir on low heat for 5-7 minutes till transparent.
4. Add cabbage and capsicum. Sauté for 2 minutes. Add ½ tsp turmeric powder and dry mango powder. Stir on low heat for 1 minute.
5. Add ¾ cup coriander, 4 tbsp of chopped mint. Stir for 1-2 minutes.
6. Add *paneer* and 4 tbsp tomato ketchup. Cook for a minute. Add salt, pepper powder, *garam masala* and red chilli powder and cook for 2-3 minutes. Add *chaat masala* to taste.
7. Lastly add the tomato fingers and mix lightly. Remove from heat.
8. Take one *roomali roti* and place it on a hot *tawa* smeared with 1 tsp oil, turn side and cook only for a few seconds (do not let it turn crisp).
9. Remove from *tawa*. Spread some hari *chutney* and ketchup mix. Place some filling on one edge, leaving 2" an the edge. Fold over, turn the left and right sides and holding on, roll to get a *kathi* roll. Serve with green chutney.

FREE HOME DELIVERY IN SOUTH DELHI
ANUP

Kadhai Paneer

Coriander seeds and dry fenugreek leaves are used to flavour this exotic dish of paneer.

Serves 4

INGREDIENTS

- 250 gms *paneer* - cut into 2" fingers
- 1 green capsicums - cut into thin 2" long strips
- 1 big onion - cut into half and then into thin slices widthwise
- 2 dry, red chillies
- 5 tbsp oil
- 1½ tsp coriander seeds (*sabut dhania*)
- ½ tbsp crushed garlic
- 1 tbsp ginger - juliennes
- 5 tomatoes
- 1 green chilli
- 2 tbsp ready made tomato puree
- 1 tsp tomato ketchup
- 1 tsp *degi mirch powder*
- 1 tsp salt, or to taste
- ¼ tsp sugar
- ½ tsp *garam masala*
- 2 tsp *kasuri methi*
- ½ cup cream

METHOD

1. Chop tomatoes and boil them in ¼ cup water along with a green chilli for 4-5 minutes, stirring on low heat till soft. Remove from fire and let them cool. Crush tomatoes to a rough puree with a hand blender or give a quick churn in a mixer.
2. Split coriander seeds into two pieces with a rolling pin. Keep aside. Dry roast *kasuri methi* on a *tawa* for 2 minutes and crush to a powder. Keep aside.
3. Heat oil. Add coriander seeds and wait till they turn golden. Add ginger juliennes, stir and add dry red chillies and stir till they start to darken. Add onions and stir till light golden. Add garlic and stir again.
4. Add freshly crushed tomatoes, ready made tomato puree and *degi mirch* powder stir fry for about 5-7 minutes till oil separates. Add ketchup, salt, sugar, *garam masala,* and roasted and powdered *kasuri* methi.
5. Add capsicum strips and stir for 2 minutes.
6. Add cream and mix well. Cook for a minute till *masala* turns reddish again.
7. Add *paneer.* Add a little water, about ¼ cup if it appears too thick. Cook for 1-2 minutes. Transfer to a serving dish. Garnish with shredded ginger. Serve hot with *paranthas.*

FREE HOME DELIVERY IN SOUTH DELHI
ANUP

taste of Rajasthan

Some of the factors that influence the cuisine of Rajasthan are: the desert climate, the ancient history, and the cultural and artistic traditions. In this climate, it is necessary to use dry ingredients like lentils, spices and various flours when vegetables and greens are scarce. Papads and badis, kept in storage, are turned into curries. Cows, goats and camels provide milk for yogurt, butter, cheese and ghee.

The art of hunting wild game was a basic necessity-driven activity which was turned into the elaborate shikar for the noble families. The manner of cooking over an open fire has been handed down through generations. In the royal forts, palaces and havelis, trained chefs perfected and refined their recipes to please their patrons. Many of these dishes have been embraced nationally and internationally, for example, in non-vegetarian, the sulas (barbecues), Laal Maans and Safed Maans. In vegetarian, the numerous dishes based on gatte, mangoris, badis, corn, millet and wheat. However the standard everyday fare still remains dal-bati-churma.

The special Water Storage tank for the Camels.

Khoye wale Shahi Gatte

They deserve to be, called Shahi, royal, because of the rich paneer and khoya stuffing in them.

Serves 4

INGREDIENTS - DOUGH

- 1¼ cups gram flour (*besan*)
- a pinch of baking soda (*mitha soda*)
- ¾ tsp cumin seeds
- ¼ tsp red chilli powder
- ½ tsp salt
- 2 tsp chopped ginger
- 1 tbsp *ghee*
- 2½ tbsp yogurt

FILLING

- 50 gms *paneer*
- 50 gms milk solids (*khoya*)
- salt to taste
- 2 green chillies - finely chopped

CURRY

- 2 tbsp oil
- 1 tsp cumin seeds (*jeera*)
- a pinch asafoetida (*hing*)
- 1 cup ready made tomato puree
- 1 cup yogurt - whisked well till smooth
- 4 tsp coriander powder
- 2 tsp red chilli powder
- 1 tsp turmeric powder
- ½ tsp *garam masala* powder

METHOD

1. Mix gram flour with all ingredients of the dough. Add some warm water to make a hard, but pliable dough. Knead well and keep aside covered.
2. For the filling, grate *khoya* and *paneer.* Mix grated *khoya*, *paneer*, chopped green chillies and a pinch of salt.
3. Divide dough into 3 portions. Roll out a portion to a 5" long oval shape and then place *khoya paneer* lengthwise in it. Carefully cover the stuffing with the dough on the sides and roll nicely to seal. Give it a cylindrical shape. Repeat this with the left over dough and filling.
4. Boil enough water in a medium deep pan so that the *gatte* can dip in water properly. Add ½ tsp salt. Add these stuffed *gatte* in boiling salted water. Boil for about 10 minutes. Remove from water when done. Keep water aside. Let them cool. Cut in to small pieces. Deep fry and keep aside.
5. For preparing curry, heat oil, add cumin seeds, when they turn golden, add tomato puree, red chilli powder, asafoetida and turmeric powder, cook until oil starts separating.
6. Mix yogurt with coriander powder. Lower the heat and add yogurt, stirring continuously. Add 1 cup water of the *gatte.* Boil. Adjust salt, add garam masala powder. Add *gatte* and cook for 2-3 minutes until gravy thickens. Serve hot.

Dal-Bati-Churma

Bati is the typical ball-shaped, baked bread and is served with spicy mixed lentils.

Serves 4

INGREDIENTS - for DAL

- ¼ cup split green *moong dal* (*moong chilka*)
- ¼ cup *channa dal*
- 1 cup split black lentils (*urad chilka*)
- ½ tsp turmeric powder
- 1 tsp salt, or to taste
- 4 tbsp oil
- 1 tsp cumin seeds
- 1 pinch asafoetida
- 2 dry red chillies whole
- 2 bay leaves (*tej patta*)
- 3 cloves (*laung*)
- 1" piece cinnamon
- 2 green cardamoms
- 5-6 curry leaves, optional
- 1 tbsp chopped ginger
- 3 green chillies - chopped
- 2 medium tomatoes - chopped
- 1 tsp red chilli powder
- ¼ cup chopped fresh coriander leaves
- 1 medium lemon

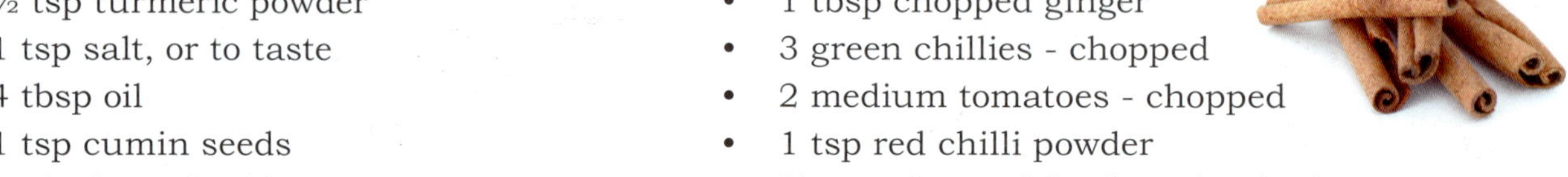

METHOD

1. Pick, wash and soak *moong chilka*, urad *chilka* and *channa dal* in about 6 cups of water for an hour. Boil the dals with turmeric and salt till done and mix them properly. Heat oil in a pan. Add cumin seeds, asafoetida, whole dry red chillies, bay leaves, cloves, cinnamon, cardamom, curry leaves, ginger, green chillies, tomatoes and red chilli powder; fry till the oil gets separated from the mixture. Add the cooked *dal* to this and blend properly. Finish off with lemon juice and chopped coriander.

INGREDIENTS - for BATI

- 2 cups whole wheat flour (*atta*)
- ½ tsp salt to taste
- 1 tsp carom seeds (*ajwain*)
- ½ cup *ghee*

METHOD

1. Mix the flour and salt. Rub *ghee* into the flour mixture till it resembles bread crumbs. Add *ajwain* and make a firm dough using water. Make small balls, flatten slightly and press with the thumb lightly in the centre. Roast them in a hot oven at 200°C for about 25-30 minutes. Take out, press lightly and soak in a bowl of *ghee.* Drain and serve with *ghee* and *dal.*

INGREDIENTS - for CHURMA

- 2 cups whole wheat flour (*atta*)
- 4 tbsp melted *ghee*
- 1 cup grated Jaggery
- 3 tbsp *ghee*

METHOD

1. Pour 4 tbsp hot *ghee* in wheat flour and mix until it looks like bread crumbs. Prepare a hard dough with about ½ cup water. Make thick *chapatis.* Prick with a fork. Bake *chapatis* at 200°C in a pre-heated oven for 20 minutes. Remove from oven and cool.
2. Make a fine powder from the cooled *chapatis* in a mixer. Melt 3 tbsp *ghee* in a *kadhai.* Add *chapati* powder and stir to mix well. Remove from heat. Add jaggery. Mix well so that jaggery lumps do not form. Serve *churma* as it is or make *laddoos* if you like. Garnish with chopped almonds and pista.

Laal Maans

A fiery red meat curry with an appetizing red colour and tempting aroma.

Serves 4-5

INGREDIENTS - DOUGH

- 800 gms lamb (mutton) - cut into pieces
- 15 whole dry, red chillies - soak in hot water for 10 mins & grind to a fine paste
- ½ cup oil
- 4-5 black cardamoms (*moti elaichi*)
- 4-5 cloves (*laung*)
- 1" cinnamon (*dalchini*)
- 4 onions - chopped
- 2 tbsp ginger paste
- 2½ tbsp garlic paste
- 1 tsp *degi mirch* powder
- ¾ cup yogurt
- 1 tsp cumin powder (*jeera*)
- 1 tbsp coriander powder (*dhania*)
- ½ tsp turmeric powder (*haldi*)
- 2 tsp salt

TEMPERING

- 2 tbsp *ghee*
- 8-10 flakes garlic - chopped
- 2-3 cloves (*laung*)

METHOD

1. Heat oil. Add black cardamoms, cloves and cinnamon. Wait for a minute.
2. Add chopped onions and sauté till brown.
3. Add mutton and sauté for 4-5 minutes. Add *degi mirch* and stir to mix well.
4. Add garlic-ginger, sauté for 2-3 minutes.
5. Beat the yogurt well and add cumin powder, coriander powder, turmeric powder, prepared red chilli paste and salt.
6. Add yogurt to mutton and stir frequently for about 5-7 minutes till oil separates.
7. Add 2 cups hot water. Bring to a boil and simmer covered on low heat for 40 minutes, stirring in between. Cook till tender.
8. Heat *ghee* in a small pan. Add garlic and cloves and when you start getting the aroma, remove from fire and add to the mutton. Cover and keep aside till serving. Serve hot with rice or *missi roti*.

Bajra Roti aur Lahsuni Chutney

Millet is transformed into a joyful masterpiece of taste and texture in these traditional recipes.

Makes 6 *rotis*

INGREDIENTS - for BAJRA ROTI

- 2 cups millet flour (*bajre ka atta*)
- 1 large potato - boiled & mashed
- ½ onion - finely chopped
- ¼ cup finely grated fresh coconut
- 3-4 green chillies - chopped
- 3-4 tbsp fresh coriander - chopped
- 1½ tsp salt
- 1 tsp dry mango powder (*amchoor*)
- 1 tsp garam masala
- 1½ tsp ginger - paste or finely chopped

METHOD

1. Mix all ingredients well to a firm, smooth dough with warm water. Apply 1 tbsp *ghee* on the dough and keep aside for 5 minutes. Divide into 6 balls. Roll a ball into a slightly thick *roti* using some millet flour. Heat *tawa* and cook *roti* on medium heat. Turn when the underside is cooked. Cook both sides. Put butter or *ghee* and serve. You can also fry *rotis* in *ghee*, pressing the *roti* lightly to cook properly as the *roti* is a little thick.

Tip: *Knead the dough as close to serving time as possible as the dough starts becoming loose on keeping. If you want to knead a couple of hours earlier, see that it is a little stiff dough.*

INGREDIENTS - for LAHSUNI CHUTNEY

- 14-15 large garlic flakes - chopped
- 2 tsp red chilli powder
- juice of one lemon
- 1½ tsp fennel seeds (*saunf*) - roasted and crushed
- ½ tsp salt, or to taste

METHOD

- Grind all the ingredients together roughly in a mixer, using a little water for grinding.

Bajre ki Khichri

Serves 4

INGREDIENTS

- 1 cup pearl millet (*bajra*) - soaked for 2-3 hours
- ¼ cup yellow *moong dal*
- 1 tbsp *ghee*
- ½ tsp pepper corns (*saboot kali mirch*)
- 2-3 cloves (*laung*), ½ tsp cumin seeds
- a pinch of asafoetida (*hing*)
- 1 green chilli - chopped
- 1 tsp chopped ginger, ¾ tsp salt
- a pinch of turmeric powder

TEMPERING

- 1 tbsp *ghee*, ½ tsp red chilli powder

METHOD

1. Drain soaked bajra and grind roughly in a mixer. Traditionally it was done in a stone crusher. Heat *ghee*, add pepper corns, cloves, cumin seeds and asafoetida. Add the washed *dal* and *bajra*. Add ginger and green chillies. Sauté for 3-4 minutes. Add 6 cups of water, salt and turmeric powder. Pressure cook till 2 whistles. Lower the heat and cook for another 6-7 minutes. To temper, heat 1 tbsp *ghee* and add red chilli powder. Pour over the hot *khichri*. Serve garnished with chopped coriander leaves.

taste of Lucknow

Under the patronage of the Nawabs of Awadh, music, dance and poetry bloomed – as did the art of cooking. In the Nawabi kitchen one cook did not cook the entire meal. There were several chefs, each with his own area of expertise. It was this intense interest in food that created the highly refined food heritage of this city. Breads include a variety of naans, sheermals, kulchas, taftans, and rumali roti. Desserts are kheer, firni, gullathi (three different ways of cooking rice with milk), sewain, muzaafar, zarda, shahi tukray and a variety of halwas.

Vegetarian fare is equally important in the Ganga-Jumni tahzeeb, the harmonious synthesis of different cultures. Paranthas, puris, plain kachoris and stuffed kachoris accompany the dishes of fresh seasonal vegetables and lentils. A major role is played by milk and milk products – malai, khoya, butter, ghee and yogurt.

Mutton, fish and chicken dishes are cooked in precise steps and with great care. Biryanis and pulaos are cooked on 'dum' i.e., the pot is tightly sealed and the ingredients cook in their own steam on low heat, ensuring a wonderful infusion of flavours and aromas. Cooking on 'dum' is a method applied in many recipes, both vegetarian and non-vegetarian.

'Galawat' means a tenderizer such as a paste of raw papaya, rubbed on meat or keema (ground meat) to make it completely soft, producing the most delectable, mouth-melting results, as found in the famous Galouti Kebab and Kakori Kebab. Other kinds of kebabs are Boti Kebabs, Patili ke kebab, Seekh Kebab and Shami Kebab.

Bara Imambara — a famous monument built by the Nawab of Awadh in 1784.

Kachori aur Chatpati Aloo Bhaji

Flaky, deep fried kachori is a delight with a potato dish.

Makes 12-14

INGREDIENTS - for KACHORI

- 2 cups plain flour (*maida*)
- 6 tbsp oil, ¼ tsp baking soda (*mitha soda*)
- ¾ tsp salt, oil for frying

FILLING

- 4 tbsp yellow *moong dal*
- a pinch of turmeric (*haldi*) powder
- 4-5 tbsp oil
- 2 pinch of asafoetida (*hing*)
- 8 tbsp gram flour (*besan*)
- 1 tbsp cumin seeds (*jeera*)
- 1 tbsp coriander seeds (*sabut dhania*)
- 2 tbsp fennel seeds (*saunf*)
- ½ tsp salt, ½ red chilli powder
- ½ tsp *chaat masala*

METHOD

1. Mix plain flour with salt, soda and oil. Rub the flour between the palms till oil is well mixed. Add 8-10 tbsp water gradually to get a slightly stiff dough. Knead well. Keep aside.
2. For the filling, roughly blend cumin seeds, fennel seeds and coriander to a coarse powder in a mixer or pestle-mortar.
3. Wash the *moong dal.* Add 2 cups water, pinch of turmeric and ½ tsp salt. Boil for 3-4 minutes till cooked but firm. Drain the water and keep aside.
4. Take a clean *kadhai.* Heat 5 tbsp oil and add the asafoetida. Add gram flour and cook for 2-3 minutes on medium heat till gram flour is light golden in colour and the raw smell of gram flour is not there. Add the coarse powder of fennel seeds, coriander, cumin seeds. Add salt, red chilli powder, *chaat masala* and boiled *moong dal.* Mix well and cook for 1-2 minutes. Keep filling aside.
5. Divide the dough in 12-14 balls. Roll out small thick *poori* and place 1 tbsp full of filling in center, pick up all Sides and seal well by pinching edges. (if not sealed well, the *kachori* will burst and absorb oil) Flatten *kachori* and roll lightly to get 2½"-3" *kachori.* Repeat with remaining dough.
6. Heat oil in a *kadhai* for frying. Add 3-4 at a time, lower heat and fry on medium heat for 7-8 minutes till crisp and light golden on both sides.
7. To serve, refry the *kachoris* in hot oil for a minute till golden brown. Serve hot with *imli chutney* or with *Aloo ki Chatpati Bhaji.*

INGREDIENTS - for CHATPATI ALOO BHAJI

- 4 potatoes - boiled, peeled and each cut into 8 pieces
- 4 large tomatoes
- 2 tsp coriander seeds (*sabut dhania*)
- 2 tsp sesame seeds (*til*)
- 1 tsp cumin seeds (*jeera*)
- 2 whole dry red chillies
- 2 onions - chopped, 1 onion - sliced
- 1½ tsp salt

GREEN PASTE

- ½ tsp red chilli powder
- 8 big flakes garlic
- 1½" piece ginger, 2-3 green chillies
- ½ cup green coriander leaves

METHOD FOR ALOO BHAJI

1. Boil whole tomatoes in 3 cups of water for 5-7 minutes. Remove from water. Cool and grind to a puree.
2. Dry roast coriander seeds, sesame seeds, cumin seeds & whole red chillies for 1-2 minutes. Cool and grind to a rough powder. Keep aside.
3. Grind garlic, ginger, green chillies and coriander leaves with ¼ cup water to a green paste.
4. Heat 6 tbsp oil in a clean *kadhai*, add the chopped onions, cook till slightly golden. Add the sliced onions and cook till golden brown. Add the green paste and cook for 4-5 minutes.
5. Add the purred tomatoes and mix well for 2 minutes. Add salt and red chilli powder and mix.
6. Now add the potatoes and the powdered dry *masala*. Mix well for 2 minutes on very low heat. Remove from heat. Serve with *kachori*.

Avadh ke Shahi Kofte

These potato and spinach koftas are simmered in delicate gravy enriched with almonds, melon seeds and poppy seeds – a marvel of tastes and aromas.

Serves 4

INGREDIENTS

KOFTAS

- 250 gms potatoes - boiled and mashed
- ¼ cup chopped coriander
- ½ cup chopped spinach (*palak*)
- ¼ cup cornflour
- 1 tbsp lemon juice
- 2 tbsp dry fenugreek leaves (*kasuri methi*)
- ½ tsp *garam masala*
- 1 tsp salt, or to taste

MASALA PASTE

- 12 almonds (*badam*)
- 4 tbsp melon seeds (*magaz*)
- 4 tbsp poppy seeds (*khus-khus*)
- 6 green chillies
- 1 onion
- ½" piece of ginger
- 3-4 flakes of garlic

OTHER INGREDIENTS

- 3 tbsp oil
- 2 onions - finely chopped
- 1 cup yogurt (*dahi*) - whisk till smooth
- ½ cup milk
- ¼ cup cream
- ½ tsp turmeric (*haldi*)
- 1 tsp sugar, 1 tsp salt
- ½ cup water

METHOD

1. Mix all ingredients of the koftas together in a bowl. Form into 1½" long rolls and deep fry 1-2 at a time in hot oil and keep aside.
2. Grind all ingredients for the *masala* paste together in a mixer to a fine paste.
3. For the gravy, heat 3 tbsp oil add chopped onions, stir till golden brown.
4. Add the ground *masala* paste and fry for a 2- 3 minutes.
5. Reduce heat, stirring continuously add yogurt, milk, cream, turmeric, sugar and salt. Bring to a boil, stirring continuously.
6. Add ½ cup water and cook for another 5 minutes. Remove from heat & keep aside till serving time.
7. At the time of serving heat up the gravy add the koftas and simmer for a minute for the *koftas* to get hot. Serve hot.

Galouti Kebab

Delicious kebabs which melt in your mouth! Must give it a try.

Makes 15 *kebabs*

INGREDIENTS - PRESSURE COOK TOGETHER

- 500 gms lamb mince (*keema*)
- ½ tsp *garam masala*
- ¼ tsp nutmeg (*jaiphal*) powder
- ¼ tsp mace (*javitri*)
- seeds of 3 black cardamoms (*moti elaichi*)
- 2" stick cinnamon (*dalchini*)

OTHER INGREDIENTS

- 1½ tbsp *kachri* powder
- ¼ tsp baking soda (*mitha soda*)
- 2 onions - cut into slices
- 2 tbsp ginger-garlic paste
- 1 egg white - separate egg yolk from egg white
- 1 tsp *tandoori masala*
- ½ tsp *garam masala*
- ½ tsp red chilli powder
- 1 tsp salt or to taste
- 4 tbsp gram flour (*besan*)
- 2 tbsp chopped coriander
- 5 tbsp melted butter
- oil for frying

METHOD

1. Wash the mince in a strainer and press out excess water.
2. Put the mince in a pressure cooker. Add ¼ tsp nutmeg, ¼ tsp mace, seeds of 3 black cardamoms, 1" stick cinnamon and ½ cup water. Give 2 whistles. Keep on low heat for 2-3 minutes. Remove from heat. The *keema* should be cooked. After the pressure drops, if there is any water, dry out the water completely on fire.
3. Place boiled mince in a mixer blender. Churn till smooth. Keep aside.
4. Heat 1 cup oil in a *kadhai* and fry the sliced onions till golden brown. Remove from oil with a slotted spoon and grind to a brown paste.
5. Add the brown onion paste, ginger-garlic paste, *kachri* powder, 1 egg white, salt, chilli powder, *tandoori masala* and *garam masala* to the mince mixture. Mix to get a sticky consistency. Remove to a bowl.
6. Roast gramflour in a *kadhai* or pan on low heat till light golden and fragrant.
7. Add roasted gram flour, chopped coriander and butter to the mince mixture. Keep for 1 hour in the refrigerator. Shape mince into flat, 4" diameter *tikkis*.
8. Shallow fry on low heat in 4 tbsp oil on a *tawa* or pan, till brown on both sides. Sprinkle some *chaat masala* and serve with onion rings mixed with some lemon juice and *dahi pudina chutney*.

Lucknow ki Khaas Degh-e-Biryani

Mutton pulao flavoured with herbs and spices.

Serves 4

INGREDIENTS

- ½ kg mutton with bone
- 2 cups basmati rice
- 2 bay leaves
- 2 black cardamoms (*moti elaichi*)
- 1 large onion and 1 green chilli - ground to a paste
- a few threads saffron - soaked in 1 tbsp *kewra* water
- ½ cup chopped coriander and ½ cup mint leaves

MARINADE

- 1 cup curd - whisked
- 3 tsp garlic paste
- 2 tsp ginger paste
- 1½ tbsp powdered almonds or almond paste
- 1½ tsp red chilli powder

GRIND TOGETHER AND ADD TO MARINADE

- seeds of 6 green cardamoms (*chhoti elaichi*)
- 4 cloves (*laung*)
- 2 blades mace (*javitri*)
- ¼ teaspoon ground nutmeg
- 2½ tsp salt, or to taste

METHOD

1. Wash meat, drain and dry.
2. Combine ingredients for marinade. Grind spices and add to the yogurt marinade. Marinate meat for atleast 30 minutes, preferably 2-3 hours.
3. Wash rice and soak for one hour.
4. Heat 5 tablespoon oil in a pressure cooker, add bay leaves and black cardamoms. After 2 minutes add onion-green chilli paste and fry till golden. Stir in marinated meat and stir for 10 minutes till brown and dry. Add 4 cups warm water. Pressure cook for 13 minutes after the first whistle on low medium heat.
5. Allow pressure to cool before opening. Check meat for tenderness.
6. Heat 3 tbsp oil in a *kadhai*. Drain rice, add to pan and stir for 3-4 minutes very gently without breaking the grains.
7. Place half the rice in a heavy bottomed *degh* or *handi*, and place all the meat pieces and about 1 cup stock/gravy on the meat.
8. Cover meat with the remaining rice and pour the rest of the gravy/stock over the top
9. Sprinkle with the saffron and *kewra* water.
10. Add the chopped coriander and mint leaves.
11. Bring the *degh* or *handi* to a boil. Cover with a well fitting lid and keep on very low heat for 15-18 minutes or till stock is absorbed and the rice is cooked.

Jalebi

Hot, crisp and perfect jalebis every time!

Makes ½ kg

INGREDIENTS - BATTER

- 1 cup flour (*maida*)
- 1¼ cups homemade curd, preferably slightly sour like 1 day old curd

SUGAR SYRUP, SEE NOTE

- 2 cups sugar
- 1½ cups water
- few strands of saffron (*kesar*)

OTHER INGREDIENTS

- ¼ tsp baking soda (*mitha soda*)
- 1 tbsp gram flour (*besan*)
- oil/*ghee* for deep frying, empty milk packet or a squeeze bottle

METHOD

1. Mix flour and 1¼ cup curd to make a thick, soft dropping consistency batter like *pakoda* batter. Add ¼ cup water if the batter appears too thick. Keep this batter covered for 1-2 hours at room temperature for fermentation. In winter, the batter should be kept in a warm place or in the sun. Do not over-ferment the batter.
2. For the sugar syrup, heat sugar and water till sugar dissolves. Add saffron. Bring to a boil. Cook for 7-8 minutes on medium heat till you get a syrup of a slight sticky consistency. Do not cook longer to get a thread consistency. Keep aside to cool down to room temperature.
3. Take a flat bottom pan, a medium size non-stick pan works well. Pour enough oil/*ghee* for frying about 1" height.
4. Add gramflour and baking soda to the batter. Mix well and spoon this batter in an empty milk packet or a squeeze bottle. If using a milk packet, after filling with batter, tie it with a rubber band and make a small cut at one corner of the packet. Thin *jalebis* will remain crisp for longer but very thin *jalebis* turn brown too fast.
5. Make *jalebi* shape directly into the medium hot *ghee*, piping from inside to outside and keeping a little distance between the rings. Pull the last ring towards the centre to lock the *jalebi*. Deep fry on medium heat for about 2-3 minutes, turning sides with tongs (*chimta*) till rich golden brown on both sides. First try one to check the thickness of your liking.
6. Take out the *jalebi* from the oil/*ghee* and immediately dip into the sugar syrup at room temperature for ½ -1 minute. Serve hot.

Note: *Sugar syrup if over cooked will form a dry coating on the jalebi. If under-cooked, it will turn the jalebis soggy. So check the syrup between the thumb and fore finger. The sugar syrup should not be hot when the jalebis are put into it. The left over sugar syrup can be transferred to a bottle and kept in the refrigerator for 5-6 weeks.*

taste of Gujarat

Gujrati cuisine is predominantly vegetarian. It follows the unique practice of adding a pinch of sugar to harmonise the spice and salt in the food. It is simple, practical and healthy. Gujrat is the biggest producer of milk in India. Protein is brought into the diet by a generous use of milk and milk products such as yogurt and butter milk. Gramflour is used to make the variety of snacks called farsan which are always kept ready to serve guests. Famous appetisers are dhokla and khandvi. A large variety of lentils form part of the diet. There are many varieties of karhis, using a yogurt-gramflour base. The vegetables used are fresh and seasonal.

There is some variation within the four geographical regions of the state. For example in Kathiawar the speciality is a spicy methi masala made with dried fenugreek leaves and chilles. Papads, pickles and chutneys accompany every meal. Sprouts and salads are another feature, making this a healthy cuisine.

Famous Rabari/Kutch embroidery of Gujrat.

Khakra

Serves 4

INGREDIENTS

- 1 cup wheat flour (*atta*)
- 1 cup plain flour (*maida*)
- 1 tsp salt, ¼ tsp turmeric powder
- 1 tsp *garam masala*
- 4 tsp *ghee*
- warm water or milk as required

METHOD

1. Sieve wheat flour, *maida,* salt, turmeric and *garam masala.* Add ghee, knead with enough warm water or milk to a soft dough. Divide into 8 balls and roll out each into very thin *rotis.* Cook *rotis on a hot tawa,* smear *ghee* on each and pile one roti on top of the other. Take 2-3 *rotis* and roast them on a hot *tawa* by pressing with a folded cloth. As each *roti* turns crisp on the under side, turn and roast the other side till brown.

Methi Thepla

Makes 8-9

INGREDIENTS

- 1 cup wheat flour
- ¼ cup curd, 1 tbsp oil
  ½ tsp chilli powder, 1 tsp salt
- ½ tsp sugar
- ¼ rsp turmeric powder (*haldi*)
- ½ cup chopped fenugreek leaves

METHOD

1. Mix all ingredients with wheat flour. Add about ¼ cup water to make a soft dough. Keep aside for 15-20 minutes.
2. Divide dough into 8-9 equal portions. Roll out each portion very thinly to get a 6" diameter *roti.* Cook on a hot *tawa* using a little oil or *ghee.* Serve either hot or cold with *chundo* (*aam ki chutney*) or in the *thali.*

Chundo

Raw mangoes are grated and soaked in salt and turmeric powder to make this chutney.

Serves 6-8

INGREDIENTS

- 4 medium (500 gms) raw mangoes
- 1½ cups (250 gms) sugar
- 2 tsp red chilli powder
- ¾ tsp turmeric (*haldi*) powder
- 1 tsp cumin powder (*jeera*)
- 2 tsp salt

METHOD

1. Peel & grate mangoes. Add salt & turmeric to grated mangoes & leave it for 3-4 hours.
2. Add sugar & cook on medium heat, stirring occasionally till it boils. Reduce heat, add chilli powder. Cook till thick. Remove from heat. Add cumin. Fill in a sterilised jar.

Khandvi

Small stuffed rolls made of gram flour cooked in buttermilk.

Serves 6-8

INGREDIENTS

- ½ cup gram flour (*besan*)
- 1¾ cups butter milk (mix ¾ cup curd with 1 cup water)
- ¼ tsp turmeric (*haldi*)
- ¼ tsp cumin seeds (*jeera*)
- ½ tsp coriander powder (*dhania*)
- a pinch asafoetida (*hing*)
- 1 tsp salt
- 1 tsp sugar
- 1 tsp ginger-green chilli paste
- 1 big (12") *thali* or tray - greased with oil

FILLING (OPTIONAL)

- 1 tbsp oil
- 2 tbsp grated carrots
- 1 tbsp grated fresh coconut

INGREDIENTS FOR TEMPERING

- 1½ tbsp oil
- ½ tsp mustard seeds
- 2-3 green chillies - diagonally sliced
- few coriander leaves
- few curry leaves

METHOD

1. Mix gram flour with buttermilk till smooth. Give one boil, remove from heat. Stir.
2. Add all other ingredients and ginger-green chilli paste. Cook for about 10-12 minutes, stirring continuously or until mixture becomes thick and translucent.
3. Immediately spread mixture thinly on back of greased *thali* or tray while it is hot. Level lightly with the back of a greased *katori.*
4. Heat 1 tbsp oil for filling. Add coconut and carrots and sauté for 2-3 minutes. Add salt to taste.
5. Cut into 3" wide strips and 9-10 inches long. Keep a small amount of filling at the edge. Roll each strip to get small cylinders.
6. Heat oil for tempering. Add mustard seeds and other ingredients and wait for a minute. Pour it on the *khandvis.*

Instant Khaman Dhokla

Yellow dhokla prepared instantly from gramflour.

Serves 6

INGREDIENTS

- 1½ cups gram flour (*besan*)
- ¾ cup water
- 1 tsp sugar
- ¼ tsp turmeric powder (*haldi*)
- 1 tsp salt
- 1 tsp green chilli paste
- 1 tsp ginger paste
- ¼ tsp baking soda (*mitha soda*)
- 1 tbsp oil
- 1½ tbsp eno fruit salt (2 sachet)
- 2 tsp lemon juice

TEMPERING

- 2 tbsp oil
- 1 tsp mustard seeds (*rai*)
- 2-3 green chillies - slit into 2 long pieces
- 1¼ cups water
- 2 tsp sugar
- ¼ cup white vinegar

METHOD

1. Sift gram flour through fine sieve to make it light and free of any lumps.
2. Mix gram flour, sugar, turmeric powder, salt, chilli-ginger paste, baking soda, oil and water to a smooth batter. Keep aside for 10-15 minutes.
3. Put 2-3 cups water in a big pan and place a ring (a loose bottom cake tin without the base works well) in it. Keep it for boiling.
4. Grease a 5-6" square cake tin with oil.
5. Add eno fruit salt to the above batter and pour lemon juice over it. Beat well for a few seconds.
6. Immediately pour this frothy mixture in the greased tin and tap lightly to level it.
7. Place the *dhokla* tin on the ring. Cover the pan and steam for 12-13 minutes on medium heat, till a knife inserted in the *dhokla* comes out clean. Remove pan from heat and leave the *dhokla* covered in it for 5 minutes in steam. Cool and cut into pieces. Carefully remove the pieces and arrange on the platter.
8. To temper, heat oil, and mustard. As it splutters, add green chillies. Add water and sugar. Bring to a boil. Remove from heat and add vinegar. Spoon the tempering on the *dhokla*, giving it time to absorb it. Sprinkle chopped coriander. Serve after a while so that the water gets absorbed and the *dhokla* turns soft.

Undhiyu

Favourite Gujarati mixed vegetable made from Surati beans (green beans), brinjals, potatoes, kand, sweet potatoes and bananas.

Serves 5-6

INGREDIENTS

- 250 gms *surati papdi* (green broad beans or *sem ki phali*)
- 100 gms (1 small) sweet potato - peeled and cut into 1" pieces
- 200 gms blue *kand* or *jimikand* - peeled and cut into 1" pieces
- 4-6 (100 gms) small brinjals
- 3-4 small (100 gms) small potatoes
- 1 banana
- a pinch of baking soda
- ½ tsp carom seeds (*ajwain*)
- ¼ tsp salt
- 6 tbsp oil
- ¼ tsp asafoetida (*hing*)
- 1 tsp carom seeds (*ajwain*)

GRIND TOGETHER TO A MASALA

- 50 gms coriander leaves - chopped (1 cup)
- 2-3 tbsp grated coconut
- 2-3 green chillies
- 1" piece ginger
- 2-3 garlic flakes
- 1 tsp *ajwain*
- 2 tbsp coriander powder (*dhania*)
- 1 tsp cumin powder (*jeera*)
- 1 tsp red chilli powder
- ½ tsp turmeric powder (*haldi*)
- 1 tsp sugar
- 1½ tsp salt
- 2 tsp lemon juice

METHOD

1. String the green broad beans (*surati papdi*), taking care not to separate the two sides. Wash the beans, sprinkle ½ tsp carom seeds, a pinch of baking soda and ¼ tsp salt. Mix well.
2. Peel blue *kand* and sweet potatoes and cut into 1" pieces.
3. Peel potatoes, wash. Make 2 criss-cross slits on the whole potatoes and brinjals also.
4. Cut the banana into 1" pieces and make a slit in each piece.
5. Grind all ingredients of the *masala* together. Mix 4 tbsp oil.
6. Fill half of this *masala* into slits of brinjals, potatoes and bananas. Spread some *masala* on the green beans also. Mix some *masala* with the *kand* and sweet potatoes too. Keep the remaining *masala* for later use.
7. Heat 6 tbsp oil in a big heavy bottomed pan, with a tight fitting lid. Add 1 tsp carom seeds and ¼ tsp asafoetida.
8. Add half the beans forming the lower layer in the pan. Next put half of the brinjals and potatoes. Lastly put a layer of half the blue *kand* and sweet potatoes.
9. Add the rest of the beans, repeating the other 2 layers of potatoes and brinjals and last of all *kand* and sweet potatoes. Add ¾ cup water. Cover tightly and cook on low-medium heat for about 15 minutes.
10. Add banana pieces and the remaining *masala*. Add ½ cup of water. Stir carefully. Cover and cook on low heat for another 10 minutes till all the vegetables become tender and oil separates. Check salt. Garnish with chopped coriander leaves and fresh grated coconut.

Shrikhand

The thick and creamy texture of drained and sweetened yogurt makes every mouthful a luscious pleasure. The subtle touches of cardamom, nutmeg and saffron heighten the enjoyment.

Serves 6

INGREDIENTS

- 1 kg yogurt (thick and fresh) of full cream milk
- 1 cup (150 gm) sugar - powdered
- ¼ tsp saffron (*kesar*) - soaked in 1 tbsp warm milk for 5 minutes
- ½ tsp green cardamom (*chhoti elaichi*) powder
- ¼ tsp nutmeg (*jaiphal*) powder
- 2 tbsp cream
- 4-5 almonds and 4-5 pistachios - sliced

METHOD

1. Tie the freshly set yogurt in a muslin cloth for 3-4 hours. In summers you can tie it in the fridge and keep an empty bowl beneath it to collect the liquid.
2. Pass this yogurt through a sieve (soup strainer) to make it smooth.
3. Add powdered sugar, cardamom, nutmeg, saffron, cream and mix well. Transfer to a serving bowl.
4. Garnish with saffron, sliced almonds and pistachios. Serve cold.

Aam Ras

Serves 4

INGREDIENTS

- 2 mangoes - preferably Alphonso
- sugar or jaggery to taste
- 2 tbsp milk
- ¼ tsp cardamom powder (optional)
- a few saffron strands - soaked in 1 tbsp hot water
- a few cashewnuts - fried

METHOD

1. Wash the Alphonso mangoes. Peel and chop them.
2. In a blender, add the chopped mango pieces and blend.
3. Add milk, cardamom powder and sugar to taste. Blend again.
4. Transfer to a serving bowl and chill. Decorate with soaked saffron strands and fried cashewnuts.

taste of Bengal

Rice production thrives in the rainfall and soil conditions of Bengal, making rice the staple food, eaten in a variety of forms, at every meal. Farmers also raise domestic cattle which ensures a good supply of milk and milk products that are an essential part of the cuisine, specially for making the famous desserts of Bengal, like Rasgulla and Sandesh.

There are six different tastes which the Bengali palate craves: sweet, sour, salty, bitter, hot and 'koshaay'. Vegetables are cooked in imaginative and delicious ways, and even the peels, stalks and leaves are used. The magic mix of five spices, panch phoran, ensures maximum flavour – cumin, fennel, fenugreek, onion seeds and black mustard seeds. In fact onion seeds, wild celery seeds (radhuni) and mustard paste (kasaundi) provide the keynote taste of many vegetable dishes. Poshto, a poppy seed paste, is a prized flavouring for vegetables and is sometimes mixed into the rice.

Nearly every community in Bengal eats fish, goat mutton, and chicken. The numerous lakes, ponds and rivers team with freshwater fish, such as rohu, hilsa and koi. At least one meal has a fish course. Almost every part of the fish is eaten, and the head is considered a special delicacy. A famous salt water fish from the river Padma, called Ilish, is prized by connoisseurs, while prawns in different sizes are brought out of the sea.

A sculptor making the Idol of Goddess Durga for famous Durga Puja held every year.

Ghugni

Dry white peas are boiled and quickly tossed with spices.

Serves 3-4

INGREDIENTS

- 1 cup dry, white peas - boiled with 2 cups water and 1 tsp salt
- 1 tomato - chopped
- ½ cup chopped onion
- 1 tsp chopped garlic
- 1 tsp grated ginger
- ½ tsp cumin seed powder (*jeera*)
- ½ tsp coriander powder (*dhania*)
- 1 tsp *garam masala*
- 1 tbsp chopped fresh coriander
- ¼ tsp salt or to taste
- 2 tbsp oil

METHOD

1. Heat 2 tbsp oil in a *kadhai.* Add onion, ginger and garlic.
2. Add chopped tomato, boiled white peas, cumin seed powder, coriander powder, *garam masala,* ¼ tsp salt and ¼ cup water. Cook for 5- 6 minutes. Remove from heat.
3. Garnish with chopped coriander and chopped onion.
4. Serve with puffed rice (*murmura*) or onion *pakoda.*

Masala Jhinga

Serves 4

INGREDIENTS

- 400 gms jumbo prawns (*jhinga*) - cleaned and deveined
- 6 tbsp oil, preferably mustard oil
- ½ tsp *panch phoran,* see note
- 1 big onion - chopped
- 2 tbsp chopped garlic
- 1 tbsp grated ginger
- 2 tomatoes - chopped
- 1 tsp cumin seed powder
- 1 tsp red chilli powder
- 1 tsp coriander powder
- ½ tsp *garam masala*
- ½ tsp salt or to taste
- ¼ tsp sugar

METHOD

1. Heat oil in a *kadhai,* add *panch phoran.* Wait for a minute. Add onion, ginger and garlic. Stir till onion turns golden.
2. Add chopped tomato, and cook till well blended. Add cumin seed powder, red chilli powder, coriander powder, *garam masala,* salt, sugar and ¼ cup water. Cook for 3-4 minutes.
3. Add prawns and stir for 3-4 minutes till they change colour and get cooked. Serve.

Note: *Panch phoran is a mixture of 5 spices - fennel, mustard, onion seeds, cumin and fenugreek seeds.*

Bengali Machcher Jhol

Machcher means fish and Jhol means a light stew, seasoned with ground spices like ginger, cumin, coriander, chilli and turmeric. A flavourful thin curry, to be eaten with rice.

Serves 4

INGREDIENTS

- 500 gms boneless fish fillets - cut into 2" pieces
- 1 tsp turmeric (*haldi*)
- ¾ tsp salt
- 6 tbsp mustard oil or any cooking oil for frying
- ½ tsp onion seeds (*kalaunji*)
- 6 dry, whole red chillies
- 4 bay leaves (*tej patta*)
- 1 big onion - chopped
- ½ cup ready made tomato puree
- 4 whole green chillies

SPICE PASTE (MIX TOGETHER)

- 1 tsp ground coriander (*dhania powder*)
- ½ tsp cumin powder (*jeera powder*)
- 1 tsp finely grated ginger
- 1 tsp turmeric (*haldi*) powder
- a pinch of red chilli powder
- 1 tsp salt
- 6 tbsp water

METHOD

1. To remove fishy odour, rub the fish well with the turmeric and salt and keep aside for 10-15 minutes.
2. Heat oil in a non-stick frying pan over medium heat. If you are using mustard oil, let it smoke a little. Remove from heat. Cool and reheat. Now put in the fish pieces and brown lightly on all sides without cooking them through, for about 1 minute on each side.
3. Gently lift the fish out of the oil and place it on a plate. Keep aside.
4. Combine all ingredients of the spice paste in a small bowl. Keep aside.
5. Heat remaining oil. Add onion seeds. After a few seconds, add dry red chillies and bay leaves. Stir for a few seconds.
6. Add onion and cook till light brown.
7. Add the spice paste and tomato puree. Saute for about 2-3 minutes till oil separates.
8. Add 2 cups of water. Give one boil.
9. Add fish and green chillies. Simmer over medium heat for 2 minutes till the fish is cooked. Serve.

Shukto

A dry Bengali dish. A unique blend of unusual vegetables.

Serves 4-5

INGREDIENTS

- 1 raw green banana - cut into 2" long fingers
- 1 small radish (*mooli*) - cut into 2" long fingers
- 2 small brinjals (*baingan*) - cut into 4 pieces lengthwise
- 2 bitter gourds (*karela*) - thinly sliced without peeling
- ½ tsp fenugreek seeds (*methi dana*)
- ¼ tsp black mustard seeds (*sarson*)
- 1 tsp salt, or to taste
- ½ tsp sugar
- 5 tbsp oil
- ½ tsp red chilli powder
- 1 tbsp hot *ghee* to pour on top

GRIND TOGETHER TO A PASTE

- 1 tbsp mustard seeds (*sarson*) - soaked in warm water for 15 minutes
- 2 tbsp poppy seeds (*khus-khus*) - soaked in warm water for 15 minutes
- 2" piece ginger - chopped

METHOD

1. Soak the mustard seeds and *khus-khus* in warm water for 15 minutes.
2. Grind the soaked mustard seeds and *khus-khus* seeds along with 2" piece of ginger in a mixer to a paste.
3. Cut bitter gourds into thin round slices. Chop banana, radish, potato and brinjal lengthwise into 2" long pieces.
4. Heat 5-6 tbsp oil in the pressure pan or a cooker and fry the brinjals till light golden. Remove brinjals from oil. Heat oil again and fry bitter gourds also. Keep the fried vegetables aside.
5. Heat the remaining oil, add ½ tsp each of fenugreek seeds and mustard seeds. When fenugreek seeds turn golden, add the banana, radish and potato and mix well. Saute for 2 minutes.
6. Add the mustard-poppy seeds paste to the vegetables and stir for 2 minutes. Add salt and sugar.
7. Add the fried brinjal and bitter gourds. Add ½ tsp red chilli powder.
8. Add ½ cup of hot water. Close the pressure cooker and cook till it is just about to give a whistle. Do not let the whistle come. Remove from heat and keep aside for 5 minutes. After 5 minutes release steam by keeping the cooker under running water for 2 minutes. (Do not let the steam release on its own. The vegetables will get over cooked). At serving time mix *ghee* or butter with the hot vegetables and serve with rice.

Kesari Sandesh

Saffron flavoured fresh cottage cheese with a divine and delicate taste and texture.

Makes 12

INGREDIENTS - CHHENA

- 1 litre full cream milk
- 2 tbsp white vinegar

OTHER INGREDIENTS

- 3 tbsp sugar
- 1 tsp flour (*maida*)
- ¼ tsp saffron (*kesar*) - dissolved in 2 tbsp hot water
- few sliced green pistachios
- a few cloves (*laung*) - optional

METHOD

1. Boil milk. Add enough vinegar to curdle the milk. As soon as the milk curdles, add 1 bottle (5-6 cups) water to the *chhena* to bring down the temperature. This prevents overcooking of the *chhena* and helps it to remain soft.
2. Immediately strain through a muslin cloth. Squeeze completely to remove excess water.
3. Add the sugar and flour to the *chhena*. Add the saffron water, keeping the strands for topping. Mix gently.
4. Cook this mixture on a very low flame in a heavy *kadhai* stirring continuously for 5-6 minutes. Keep spreading the *chhena* on the sides of the *kadhai*, as the centre bottom of the *kadhai* gets the maximum heat. It is cooked on very low heat and with continuous stirring. If the *chhena* gets over heated, fat will separate and it will get grainy. Remove the *kadhai* from the flame at regular intervals so as not to overheat the sandesh. The sandesh mixture is ready when neither too dry not to moist.
5. Remove from heat. Put in a plate to cool. Mash with the palm. If needed, add 1-2 tsp milk gradually.
6. Shape into flat discs of ½" thickness. Press a finger on *kesar* strand and put on each sandesh. You can also put the chhena in moulds of different shapes, like the pineapple mould. Stick a clove for the stem and sliced pistachios as the leaves as shown in the picture. You can also add colour to the mixture and make triangles as shown by using a triangular mould. Draw lines by dipping a tooth pick in colour and make impression on each piece.

Rasgulla

Light and airy, heavenly balls of fresh cottage cheese in scented sugar syrup.

Makes 10

INGREDIENTS - CHHENA

- 1 litre cows milk (available in packets too)
- 2 tbsp white vinegar
- a muslin cloth spread over a big strainer

SUGAR SYRUP

- 3 cups sugar
- 1½ cups water
- 1 *ritha* broken into pieces - soak half in ¼ cup water
- 1/8 cup milk and 1/8 cup water mixed together
- 2-3 drops *kewra* essence

METHOD

1. To prepare the *chhena*, boil the milk in a heavy deep pan. Remove from heat. Stir for 2 minutes to bring down the temperature. In the meanwhile line a colander (big strainer) with muslin cloth and place over a deep pan. Place this in the wash basin.
2. To the milk, add 2 tbsp vinegar slowly and stir very gently so that the *chhena* does not disintegrate. The milk will curdle and the whey will get separated. If needed you can add a little more vinegar.
3. Once the *chhena* is done, immediately strain *chhena* through the prepared strainer (colander) lined with muslin cloth and kept over an empty pan. Keep the tap water running on the *chhena* while straining it. As the tap water falls on it, the hot water overflows from the pan beneath. Keep doing this till the *chhena* cools down completely. Till *chhena* cools completely, it should always be soaked in water else it turns chewy.
4. Strain the cooled *chhena* through a muslin cloth and squeeze gently by twisting the cloth lightly. You will get 180-200 gm *chhena* from 1 litre milk. Spread a cloth napkin on a serving tray and spread the *chhena* on the cotton cloth for 4-5 minutes to soak the excess water.
5. In the meanwhile make sugar syrup. Take a big, deep *kadhai* of about 12" diameter and 5" depth. If the *kadhai* is not big and deep, the sugar syrup boils over as the syrup needs to be frothing all the time when the *rasgullas* are boiling. Put sugar and water in the *kadhai* and cook till sugar dissolves and syrup comes to a boil. Boil on high heat for 2-3 minutes till syrup turns sticky.
6. Add milk mixed with water to the sugar syrup and without stirring, let it keep boiling and frothing on medium flame for 2-3 minutes. The frothing stops and now dirt separates and comes to the surface and sides forming a grey layer. Add ¼ cup water very slowly from the side of the pan to bring down the temperature of the sugar syrup and settle the dirt on the top. Gently remove the grey layer using a slotted spoon (*pauni*). Remove syrup from heat. Keep aside.
7. Mash the *chhena* for 3-4 minutes till almost smooth on a flat surface with your palm. Do not over do it, as it will leave *ghee*. Make 10 smooth balls.
8. Keep the cleaned syrup back on high flame. Let the syrup come to a good boil. Now add 2-3 tbsp *ritha* water and boil again which adds a lot of froth to the boiling syrup. Drop all the *chhena* balls into the frothing syrup. Let them boil on high flame for 4-5 minutes. While boiling the syrup, if the froth seems to overflow, keep swirling a flat spoon on the syrup to push the froth down without disturbing the *rasgullas*. After 4-5 minutes you can turn the *rasgullas*. Now put about ¼ cup water from the side and keep on boiling on high flame.

Lightly press the froth down with the back of the *kadchhi.* While boiling add water after every 2 minutes and lightly press the froth down. ¼ cup water at a time is added 3 more times. Total cooking time of *rasgullas* is about 10-12 minutes. It is very important that syrup should froth continuously, so never reduce the heat and take a big-medium *kadhai.*

9. Take water in a pan. Take out all the *rasgulla* from the syrup and drop them into the tap water to wash off the excess syrup. Allow these *rasgulla* to cool down for 10 minutes in the tap water.
10. In the mean while add 1 cup water to the remaining syrup to thin it down as the final syrup is never too sweet. Bring to a boil. Boil on high heat for 2 minutes. If the syrup appears dirty, strain into a clean deep pan through a muslin. Add *kewra* essence.
11. Pick up one *rasgulla* at a time from water and squeeze gently and carefully with your hands to drain out all the water. Put these *rasgulla* into the thin *kewra* sugar syrup which should not be too hot but just warm for the *rasgullas* to absorb the syrup well. Allow the *rasgulla* to soak in the syrup for about 10-15 minutes or longer. Serve.

Note: *Choose a big kadhai with a round bottom. If the kadhai has a flat bottom, the rasgullas do not move well in the syrup and need to be turned. They also acquire a flattish shape instead of a proper round. Do not reduce the sugar syrup quantity. Although quite a bit is left over, you can always store it in the fridge and reuse as required.*

taste of Mumbai

Mumbai has had its own tumultuous journey from fishing village to mega city of the 21st Century.

As successive waves of migrants came here from different parts of India to seek their fortune, they brought with them their own culture and cuisine. In Mumbai you will find the local Maharashtrian kitchens and also the Gujrati, Goan, South Indian, Muslim, Parsi and Coastal kitchens. Fish, mutton, chicken are as popular as vegetarian fare. Chicken cooked with cashews is a well known favourite. But it is the Street Food that best represents this buzzing, energetic city. Food stalls are found at every street corner, serving freshly made, hot and hearty snack-type meals. Famous among them are Batata Vada, Poha with Peanuts, Bhel Puri, Samosa, Sabudana Vada, Pao Bhaji, and Vada Pao. Among the best loved sweets are Puran Poli, and Modak, which is associated with the festival of Ganesh Chaturthi that is celebrated with great fanfare in Mumbai.

Gateway of India in Mumbai.

Chowpatty ki Bhel

Serves 3-4

INGREDIENTS

- 2 cups puffed rice (*murmura*)
- 4-5 *papdis* - roughly break into pieces
- 2 tsp roasted peanuts (*moongphali*) - split into 2 with a *chakla belan*
- 1 small potato - boiled and chopped
- 1 small onion - chopped finely
- 1-2 green chillies - remove seeds and chop finely
- 1 tsp *chaat masala*
- ¼ tsp black salt (*kala namak*)
- 2 tbsp green chutney
- 3-4 tbsp tamarind chutney

RED GARLIC CHUTNEY

- 1 whole pod garlic
- 6-8 dry red chillies
- 1 tbsp vinegar

GARNISH

- 1-2 tbsp chopped green coriander
- 4 tbsp fine *namkeen sev* (ready-made)

METHOD

1. For the *chutney*, soak peeled flakes of 1 whole pod garlic with 6-8 dry red chillies in 1 cup warm water for 15 minutes. Drain and blend them with 1 tbsp of vinegar to a paste. Add enough water for grinding to get a *chutney* consistency. Add salt to taste.
2. Dry roast the *murmura* (puffed rice) in a *kadhai* for 10 minutes on medium flame, stirring continuously, but do not let it turn brown. This makes the *murmura* crunchy and crisp.
3. Combine all the ingredients in a large bowl mixing, adding about 1 tbsp of red garlic *chutney*. Mix well. Serve immediately garnished with coriander and fine *namkeen sev*.

Mumbai ka Kala Khatta

Makes 1

INGREDIENTS

- 2 cups ice cubes
- 1 wooden ice cream stick
- 1 large kulfi mould
- ¼-½ cup *kala khatta* syrup, available readymade
- ½-1 tsp lemon juice or to taste
- ¼ tsp roasted cumin powder (*bhuna jeera*)
- a pinch of black salt (*kala namak*)

METHOD

1. In the serving glass, put *kala khatta* syrup, lemon juice, roasted cumin powder and rock salt. Keep aside.
2. Put ice cubes in an ice-shaver to get shavings of ice. Put this in a *kulfi* mould and insert an ice cream stick in it. Press the ice well to bind and make a cone of ice.
3. Put 2-3 tbsp of ice shavings in the prepared *kala khatta* syrup in the glass. Stir to mix.
4. Put the ice cone in the *kala khatta* syrup glass and serve.

Ragda Pattise

Potato tikkis topped with a delicious lentil gravy.

Serves 4

INGREDIENTS - PATTISE

- 6 medium size potatoes (½ kg) - boiled & mashed
- 3 tsp cornflour
- 1 tsp salt, or to taste

RAGDA

- 1 cup dry peas (*matar*) - soaked overnight
- ½ tsp mustard seeds (*rai*)
- a pinch of asafoetida (*hing*)
- 1 onion - finely chopped
- a few curry leaves
- 1 tbsp oil
- 1" piece ginger and 3-4 garlic flakes - crushed to a paste (1½ tsp paste)
- ½ tsp turmeric powder (*haldi*)
- 1 tsp red chilli powder
- 1 tsp cumin powder (*jeera*)
- 2 tsp coriander powder (*dhania*)
- 1½ tsp salt, or to taste
- 1 tsp *garam masala*

TO SERVE

- some green chutney
- some date & tamrind (*khajur-imli*) chutney
- some chopped coriander and finely chopped onion, optional

METHOD

1. To prepare the *pattise,* mix potatoes with cornflour and salt. Make 8 big lemon-sized balls. Flatten the balls slightly. Heat 4 tbsp oil in a frying pan or *tawa* and shallow fry them till brown and crisp.
2. To prepare the *ragda,* drain the water from the peas and pressure cook peas with 1½ cups water. After the first whistle, keep on slow fire for 10 minutes. Remove from heat.
3. Heat 2 tbsp of oil. Add mustard seeds. Let it splutter.
4. Add asafoetida, chopped onion and stir fry for 2 minutes. Add curry leaves and ginger-garlic paste. Stir fry till onion turns light brown.
5. Add turmeric, red chilli powder, cumin powder and coriander powder. Mix and add 1 cup water.
6. Add boiled peas and salt. Simmer for 5-7 minutes. Add garam masala, mix and remove from heat.
7. To serve, place 2 fried pattise in a plate. Pour 4 tbsp ragda over it. Pour a spoonful of green chutney and a spoonful of tamarind *chutney*. Garnish with chopped coriander leaves and finely chopped onion.

Misal Pav

A healthy snack made with sprouts and served with bread.

Serves 2

INGREDIENTS

- 1 cup *matki/moth* bean sprouts
- 1 potato - peeled and chopped
- 1 small tomato - chopped
- 1 tbsp oil
- ½ onion - chopped
- 1 tsp garlic paste
- ½ tsp turmeric powder
- 1 tsp *goda masala*
- 1 tsp red chilli powder
- 1 tsp tamarind pulp
- 1 tsp jaggery
- ¾ tsp salt, or to taste
- 1 tbsp freshly grated coconut
- 1 tbsp chopped coriander
- *pav* to serve

GARNISH

- ½ cup *sev*
- ½ onion - very finely chopped
- 1 tbsp chopped coriander

METHOD

1. Pressure cook sprouts, potato, tomato with ½ cup water to allow one whistle. Remove from heat. Let the pressure drop by itself.
2. Heat oil. Add onions and garlic paste.
3. Let the onions soften a little. Add turmeric powder, chilli powder and goda masala.
4. Add boiled sprout-potato mixture and 1½ cups water.
5. Add salt, tamarind pulp, jaggery, coconut and coriander. Let it simmer for 5-7 minutes. Leave a little gravy.
6. Garnish with fine sev, chopped onion and coriander. Serve with pav and a lemon wedge.

Falooda

Enjoy it as a drink or a dessert.

Serves 6

INGREDIENTS

- 1 small packet *falooda*
- 4 cups milk
- 2 tbsp sugar
- ½ cup rose syrup or *Rooh Afza*
- 6 scoop vanilla ice cream
- 2 tbsp basil (*subzah*) seeds or *tookmalanga* (black oval seeds which when soaked develop a greyish, translucent, slippery coat)

METHOD

1. Soak the *subzah* seeds in 1 cup milk. Chill the seeds in milk for about 30 minutes or even more till they swell.
2. Soak *falooda* in hot water for about 5 minutes until soft. Drain. Mix with 4 tbsp *Rooh Afza.* Keep covered in the refrigerator till serving time.
3. Add 2 tbsp sugar to the remaining 3 cups milk. Keep in the fridge to chill.
4. To serve, mix the milk with *subzah* seeds and whip well to mix the seeds. Divide it into 6 glasses.
5. Add some *falooda* in all the glasses.
6. Then gently pour in 2 tbsp *Rooh Afza* in each glass which being heavier will settle to the bottom.
7. Float a scoop of ice cream on top of each glass. Mix gently. Serve.

taste of Goa

Goa has a hot and humid climate for most of the year. Its long coastline has palm-fringed beaches, coves, bays and estuaries, making it a tourist paradise.

Rice is the staple food. The Portuguese settlers brought potatoes, tomatoes, pineapples, guavas, cashews and most important of all, chilli peppers, from their colony in Brazil to plant in Goa. These plants adapted and thrived in Goa and became an indispensable part of the food. Goa is famous for its sea food, the classic dish being Goan Curry and rice. Some popular fish are pomfret, shark, tuna and mackerel. They can be cooked in many different ways. One method, called Balchao, is like pickling, and can be made days in advance.

The Christian community enjoys pork in dishes such as Sorpotel and Vindaloo where there is a strong mix of Portuguese ingredients like vinegar with typical local Goan ingredients. A well known Goan dessert is Bebinca – layer upon layer of mouth-watering coconut pancakes. Another dessert is Dodol, made of rice flour, coconut milk, jaggery and cashew nuts.

A famous beach in Goa.

Spicy Goan Crab Soup

A coconut based soup, flavoured delicately with paprika, cumin and coriander.

Serves 4

INGREDIENTS

- 500 gm crab meat (half brown and half white)
- 2 tbsp butter
- 1" piece ginger - peeled and grated
- 1 green chili - seeded and finely chopped
- 2 garlic cloves - crushed
- ½ large onion - roughly chopped
- 2 teaspoons coriander seeds (*saboot dhania*)
- 1 tsp cumin seeds (*jeera*)
- 2 tsp paprika
- ¼ tsp turmeric powder
- 1 tsp salt, or to taste
- 1½ cups (300 ml) coconut milk
- 1 tbsp chopped fresh coriander leaves

METHOD

1. Crush the coriander and cumin seeds to a rough powder.
2. Melt the butter in a saucepan. Add the ginger, chili, garlic and onion, then cook, stirring, for 3 minutes.
3. Add crushed coriander-cumin, paprika and turmeric.
4. Stir well, then mix in the crab meat and 600 ml (3 cups) water. Bring the soup to the boil, reduce the heat and simmer for 10 minutes.
5. Add coconut milk and simmer for a further 10 minutes. Stir in the salt and chopped coriander leaves, then serve immediately.

Fish Curry

Another landscape, another cuisine – this curry has tamarind and coconut milk, curry leaves and black mustard seeds.

Serves 4

INGREDIENTS

- 400 gms of any firm white fish - cut into 2” pieces
- 4 tbsp oil
- 2-3 green chillies - de-seeded and sliced
- 1 tsp red chilli powder
- 2 tsp coriander (*dhania*) powder
- ½ tsp *garam masala*
- 1 tsp salt
- 2 cups thick coconut milk
- 2 tbsp tamarind (*imli*) pulp, optional
- 1 cup water

PASTE

- 1 medium onion
- 2½” piece of ginger
- 8-10 flakes of garlic

TEMPERING *(TADKA)*

- 2 tbsp oil
- 1 tsp black mustard seeds (*sarson seeds*)
- 8-10 curry leaves
- 3 whole, dry red chillies

METHOD

1. Make a paste of onion, ginger and garlic.
2. Heat oil in a *kadhai*, add onion paste and green chillies. Cook until onion turns brown.
3. Add red chilli powder, coriander powder, garam masala and salt. Mix. Cook on medium heat until oil separates. Sprinkle a little water if the *masala* sticks to the pan.
4. Add tamarind pulp, coconut milk and 1 cup of water. Let it come to a boil. Add fish and cook on low heat for 10-12 minutes or until the fish is cooked. Remove from heat.
5. For the tempering, heat oil in a frying pan add all the ingredients. When the seeds start spluttering, pour over the hot fish. Serve hot.

Goanese Chicken

Chicken curry with tamarind and coconut.

Serves 6

INGREDIENTS

- 800 gms chicken - cut into 12 pieces
- 6 tbsp oil
- 2 medium sized onions - finely chopped
- salt to taste
- 2 cups water
- 1 tbsp tamarind (*imli*) pulp
- ¼ tsp nutmeg (*jaiphal*) - grated

DRY ROASTED MASALA PASTE

- 1 cup grated fresh coconut
- 4-6 flakes of garlic
- 2" stick of cinnamon (*dalchini*)
- 6 cloves (*laung*)
- 4 dry red chillies (*sukhi lal mirch*)
- ½ tsp turmeric powder (*haldi*)
- 2 tbsp poppy seeds (*khus-khus*)
- 1 tsp carom seeds (*ajwain*)
- ½ tsp cumin seeds (*jeera*)
- 10 peppercorns (*sabut kali mirch*)
- 1 tsp fennel seeds (*saunf*)
- 2 star anise (*chakri phool*)
- 1½ tbsp coriander seeds (*sabut dhania*)

METHOD

1. Dry roast all ingredients of the *masala* paste together in a pan - coconut, garlic, cinnamon, cloves, whole red chillies, turmeric powder, poppy seeds, carom seeds, cumin seeds, peppercorns, fennel seeds, star anise and coriander seeds for 1-2 minutes. Remove. Cool. Grind to a paste with ¾ cup of water.
2. Heat oil in a *kadhai*/wok, add onions cook till brown.
3. Add the prepared *masala* paste and cook for 2 minutes.
4. Add the chicken pieces and sauté for 7- 8 minutes.
5. Add 2 cups of water and salt. Bring to a boil. Lower heat and cook covered for 5 minutes, or till chicken turns tender.
6. Add tamarind pulp, grated nutmeg and mix well. Cook for a minute. Serve hot with steamed rice.

Prawn Vindaloo

The wide spread belief is that Vindaloo owes its origins to the Portuguese in colonial India. It was traditionally a Potato, Pork and Vinegar curry from Goa. I feel, Vin, relates to Wine or Vinegar and Aloo is Indian for Potato. In Indian homes today, the term Vindaloo is indicative of the strength or heat of the curry. It usually has diced potatoes in sauce along with the chosen meat or chicken.

Serves 2

INGREDIENTS

- 4 medium prawns (125 gms approx.) - shelled and de-veined
- 1 small potato - cut into ½" cubes
- 1 onion - sliced
- few curry leaves
- 1 tomato - finely sliced
- ¾ tsp chilli powder
- ¼ tsp turmeric (*haldi*)
- ½ tbsp *Kashmiri* chilli powder (*degi mirch*)
- 4 tbsp oil

GRIND TO A PASTE

- 2 prawns (60 gms approx.)
- 1" piece of ginger
- 6-8 flakes of garlic (2 tbsp)
- ¼ tsp cumin (*jeera*)
- 2 tbsp vinegar

GARNISH

- 1 tbsp chopped coriander leaves

METHOD

1. Grind 2 prawns to a paste with the other ingredient. Keep aside.
2. Heat 4 tbsp oil in a *kadhai.* Add onions and curry leaves. Fry till onions turn brown.
3. Add potato, stir for a minute.
4. Add prawn paste of step 1, mix well and cook for 3-4 minutes.
5. Add chilli powder, turmeric and *degi mirch.* Cook for 2-3 minutes.
6. Add tomatoes and stir fry for 1 minute.
7. Add prawns and ½ tsp salt. Cook for 1 minute.
8. Add ¾ cup water. Give an open boil. Check if prawns are cooked. Check salt and remove from heat.
9. Serve garnished with chopped coriander leaves, along with steamed rice.

Mushroom Xacuti

Prepare xacuti masala paste as given and enjoy chicken xacuti in the same masala.

Serves 2-3

INGREDIENTS

- 200 gm mushrooms - each cut into 4 pieces
- 1 onion - finely chopped
- ½ onion - sliced
- 3 tbsp oil
- 2 tbsp tamarind pulp
- a pinch nutmeg -grated
- 1 tsp salt, or to taste

XACUTI MASALA PASTE

- ½ cup grated fresh coconut
- 2 flakes of garlic
- ¾" stick cinnamon
- 2 cloves
- 1 dry red chilli
- ¼ tsp turmeric powder
- 1 tbsp poppy seeds
- ½ tsp carom seeds
- ¼ tsp cumin seeds
- 4 peppercorns
- ½ tsp fennel seeds
- ½ star anise
- ¾ tbsp coriander seeds

METHOD

1. Dry roast all ingredients of the xacuti *masala* paste together in a pan - coconut, garlic, cinnamon, cloves, whole red chilli, turmeric powder, poppy seeds, carom seed, cumin seeds, pepper corns, fennel seeds, star anise and coriander seeds for 2-3 minutes. Remove and cool.
2. In a pan put 3 tbsp oil and fry the sliced onion till golden brown. Remove from oil. Grind the fried onions along with roasted *masala* to a paste with ¼ cup water till smooth.
3. In the same pan. Add chopped onion and cook till soft.
4. Add mushroom and sauté for 5-6 minutes on medium flame till mushrooms turns light brown.
5. Add ½ cup water and salt. Bring to boil and cook covered for 5 minutes.
6. Add prepared *masala* paste and about 1 cup water. Bring to boil and cook again for 4-5 minutes on medium flame.
7. Add tamarind pulp and boil again. Add grated nutmeg and mix well. Cook for a minute. Serve hot.

taste of Hyderabad

When the Mughal armies came to Hyderabad there was a clash of cuisines – the Mughal cuisine from cool northern regions, a blend of Persian and Turkish, with the strong and spicy, hot and bold local food. It is a good example of the interaction of cultures resulting in exciting achievements.

The local Telengana cuisine has two outstanding ingredients – tamarind and hot chillies. Other souring agents, besides tamarind, are raw mango, lemon, vinegar, yogurt and tomatoes. Tomato Kut and Mirchi ka Salan are well-loved examples of food that has a sharp sour taste but in the right balance. Another famous dish, Baghaare Baigan, is in the category of Safar ka Khaana, or food that keeps well when one is travelling.

Hyderabad is known for its Biryanis made of fine rice cooked with mutton or chicken, and its range and variety of breads, such as the slightly sweet sheermal. Haleem and other meat or chicken based dishes add to the fame of this cuisine. Stewed Apricots (Khubani), Muzaafar, Badaam ki jal, and Double ka Meetha are some well known desserts.

The Char Minar

Parda Subz Biryani

A rice biryani which is covered with thinly rolled out flour dough and baked in the oven for the flavours to blend.

Serves 4

INGREDIENTS - PARDA
- 1 cup plain flour (*maida*)
- 2 tbsp *ghee*
- ¾ tsp salt
- ½ cup milk, approx. to make a dough of rolling consistency

VEGETABLE LAYER
- 4 tbsp *ghee*
- 3 onions - sliced finely
- 2 tbsp ginger-garlic paste
- 1 cup diced carrots (¼" cubes)
- ½ cup chopped beans
- 1 cup small florets of cauliflower
- ½ cup peas
- 1 cup thick yogurt mixed with 2 tsp coriander powder
- 1¾ tsp salt, or to taste

RICE LAYER
- 2 cups rice
- 4 green cardamoms
- 1 bay leaf
- 2 whole star anise
- 2 tsp salt

GRIND TO A POWDER
- 2" piece cinnamon
- 3-4 cloves, 5 green cardamoms
- 1 blade mace (*javitri*)

FLAVOURING
- ¼ cup warm milk mixed with 2 drops of *kewra* essence & a few strands of saffron (*kesar*)
- 1 onion - sliced and deep fried till crisp
- ¼ cup mint
- 2 tbsp melted butter or *ghee*

METHOD
1. For the *parda*, mix plain flour with *ghee* & salt. Knead very well, using milk to make a smooth *roti* dough. Keep aside covered for 1 hour with a cling wrap or moist cloth.
2. For the vegetable layer, heat *ghee* in a pan, add sliced onions and sauté till brown. Add ginger-garlic paste and the ground spice powder. Stir for a few seconds. Add vegetables, stir for 5 minutes on medium flame. Reduce heat and slowly add the yogurt mixed with coriander powder, stirring constantly. Stir till yogurt dries and coats the vegetables. Add 1 cup water. Cover and cook on low heat till vegetables are crisp tender. Mix salt. Remove from heat. (The vegetable mixture should not be dry, it should have some gravy).
3. For the rice layer, boil 10 cups water with all the spices and salt in a large pan. Add rice and boil till soft but firm. Drain and spread in a large tray to cool slightly and evaporate the steam. Fluff with a fork in between.
4. To assemble the *biryani*, take a heat prof dish or *handi*. Put half of the cooked vegetables in it & cover vegetables with rice. Sprinkle milk to which *kewra* and saffron has been added. Sprinkle some fried onions & mint. Repeat the vegetable & then rice layer. Sprinkle the gravy of the vegetables on the rice. Spread onion-mint layer. Dot with 1 tbsp of melted butter or *ghee.*
5. For the *parda*, put some flour on the kitchen platform, roll out the dough thinly, slightly larger than the mouth of the *handi* or dish. Place *roti* on the dish or *handi* and seal the edges by pressing it against the sides of the dish/*handi*. Apply melted *ghee* or butter on top. Put the rice in the oven for 20-30 minutes at 160°C for "*Dum*" till the dough is light golden in colour and well cooked. To serve, cut the *parda* from the centre.

Mirch ka Salan

Mirchi ka Salan is whole green chillies in a tamarind-peanut gravy.

Serves 4-5

INGREDIENTS

- 250 gms large green chillies - make a slit on one side
- 4 medium onions - cut each into 4-6 pieces
- 2 small lemon size balls of tamarind - soak in 1 cup warm water for 15 minutes
- 1½ tbsp chopped ginger
- 2 tbsp chopped garlic
- 1 tbsp coriander seeds (*sabut dhania*)
- 1 tsp cumin seeds (*jeera*)
- 3 tbsp sesame seeds (*til*)
- ¼ cup roasted peanuts
- 1½ tsp poppy seeds (*khus-khus*)
- 2" piece dry coconut (*copra*) - thickly sliced
- a pinch fenugreek seeds (*methi dana*)
- 1 tsp red chilli powder
- 1 tsp salt
- ¼ tsp turmeric powder
- 1 tsp jaggery or sugar
- a few curry leaves

METHOD

1. Mash tamarind. Strain to get tamarind water.
2. Heat 1 tbsp oil in a pan. Add onions and roast the onions for 8-10 minutes till they soften and turn golden-brown. Remove from pan. Keep aside.
3. In the same pan dry-roast together - coriander seeds, sesame seeds, peanuts, cumin seeds, poppy seeds, *copra* and the fenugreek seeds till they darken slightly and smell roasted.
4. Grind together the onions, roasted spices, ginger and garlic, salt, turmeric, red chilli powder and jaggery/sugar in a mixer to a fine paste. Add tamarind water to the mixer and again churn till smooth. Keep aside.
5. Heat about a cup of oil in *kadhai*, and deep fry green chillies. As soon as the green chillies acquire a few golden-brown spots, remove from the pan and keep aside.
6. Heat 4 tbsp oil in a *kadhai,* add curry leaves to the oil and after a few seconds, add ground paste. Cook for about 8-10 minutes on medium flame.
7. Add the green chillies. Cook over medium heat for 3-4 minutes, stirring occasionally. Add ½ cup water if the gravy appears too thick. Bring to a boil. Cook for another 4-5 minutes on slow flame till the oil comes to the surface.

Tamatar Kut

A seasoned tomato curry which is tempered with distinctly Southern spices.

Serves 4-5

INGREDIENTS

- 1 kg ripe, red tomatoes - roughly chopped
- 1 tsp ginger paste
- 1 tsp garlic paste
- ¼ tsp fenugreek seeds (*methi dana*)
- 1 small bunch of curry leaves
- 1 tsp cumin seeds - roasted and ground (*bhuna jeera*)
- 3 onions - sliced
- 1 tsp red chilli powder
- ¼ tsp turmeric powder (*haldi*)
- 1½ tsp salt, or to taste
- 1 tbsp sesame seeds (*til)* - roasted and coarsely ground
- 2 tbsp gram flour (*besan*) - roasted to a light golden brown
- 5-6 tbsp oil

TEMPERING *(BAGHAAR)*

- ½ tsp cumin seeds (*jeera*)
- ½ tsp mustard seeds (*sarson*)
- ¼ tsp fenugreek seeds (*methi dana*)
- ¼ tbsp nigella seeds (*kalaunji*)
- 7-8 dry whole red chillies
- a few curry leaves
- 6 tbsp oil

METHOD

1. Pressure cook the tomatoes with 1½ cups water, ½ tsp each of ginger and garlic, curry leaves, ¼ tsp fenugreek seeds and roasted cumin powder for 4-5 minutes after the pressure forms. Remove from heat and let the pressure drop by itself. Sieve through a strainer to get a fine tomato puree.
2. Heat oil. Fry the onions till golden brown. Add the remaining ginger and garlic and fry for a minute. Add the tomato puree, salt, turmeric, red chilli powder and the roasted and crushed sesame seeds.
3. Blend the roasted gram flour with a little water and add to the tomatoes. Simmer for about 10 minutes over medium heat. Add a little water, if required, to attain a thick soup like consistency.
4. For tempering, heat oil. Reduce heat. Add the ingredients of the tempering. When whole red chillies turn brown, add the tempering to the tomato mixture and cover. Serve hot.

Haleem

A savoury porridge of ground meat and cracked wheat. The roadside eateries all over the city, are seen offering Haleem for iftar, when the day-long fast is formally broken. The word Haleem means mild and the dish is gentle on the system, especially after a day-long fast.

Serves 5-6

INGREDIENTS

- 1 cup cracked wheat (*dalia*)
- 500 gms boneless mutton - cut into 1" pieces
- 4 large onions - thinly sliced
- ½ tsp ginger paste
- 1 tsp garlic paste
- ¼ tsp turmeric (*haldi)* powder
- 1 tsp red chilli powder
- 1½ tsp salt, or to taste
- 1 cup yogurt, whisked
- 6-7 tbsp oil
- ¼ tsp *garam masala*
- 4-5 tbsp lemon juice
- 2 green chillies - finely chopped
- a few mint leaves

METHOD

1. Boil *dalia* in about 2 cups water till soft. Strain the excess water if any. Cool the *dalia* in the strainer to drain off all the water. Grind in mixer. Keep aside.
2. Heat oil in a pressure cooker. Add onions and cook for 5-7 minutes till light brown. remove half the onions and keep aside.
3. Add ginger-garlic paste to the remaining onions and cook for 1-2 minutes. Add salt, chilli powder and turmeric powder, sprinkle a little water and cook for a minute.
4. Add meat and fry well till the liquid dries up. Add ½ cup water and yogurt and pressure cook to allow 2-3 whistles. Reduce heat and keep on low heat for 10 minutes for the meat to get tender. Let the pressure drop by itself.
5. Open the cooker and cook for 5-6 minutes on high flame till all the moisture is absorbed by the mutton.
6. Cool and grind the cooked meat in mixer.
7. Add ground meat mixture to the ground wheat and cook on medium heat for 5-10 minutes. Add the *garam masala* and lemon juice. Garnish with fried onions, finely chopped green chillies and fresh mint leaves. Serve hot.

Mutton-Bhindi ka Shorva

A thin and soupy curry with a vegetable invariably added to it. The shorva has an attractive red colour. A few marrow bones are a must in the making of all shorvas.

Serves 4-5

INGREDIENTS

- ½ kg mutton - cut into medium size pieces
- 250 gms okra (*bhindi*) - wash, pat dry and slice off the head
- 1 big lemon size ball of tamarind - soaked in 1 cup hot water for 15 minutes
- 3 onions - thinly sliced
- ½ tsp ginger paste
- ½ tsp garlic paste
- 1 tsp red chilli powder
- ¼ tsp turmeric powder
- 1½ tsp salt
- 2 tbsp yogurt, whisked till smooth
- a pinch of *garam masala* powder
- ¼ cup green coriander chopped
- ¼ cup oil

METHOD

1. Soak tamarind in about 1 cup water for 15 minutes. De-seed, mash and strain to get tamarind water. Keep aside.
2. Slice the head off the okra. Heat oil for deep frying. Fry the okra lightly, retaining the green colour. Keep aside.
3. Heat ¼ cup oil in a pressure cooker, fry the onions on medium heat till golden brown. Put in the ginger and garlic and fry for 1-2 minutes. Add salt, turmeric and red chilli powder. Sprinkle a little water for the spices to blend well. Stir.
4. Add mutton and fry for 5-7 minutes. Add 1½ cups water and pressure cook, till the meat is tender. It takes about 2-3 whistles and then 10 minutes on medium flame for the mutton to get done.
5. Let the pressure drop by itself. When the mutton is cooked properly, add half of the tamarind water, yogurt, deep fried okra and a little additional water, if needed and bring the dish to a boil. Cook covered on slow fire till the okra is cooked through. Check the sourness of the *shorva* and add more tamarind water as needed. Bring to a boil. Sprinkle *garam masala* and serve hot.

Sheermal

A rich bread made with milk and fragrant kewra water.

Makes 12

INGREDIENTS

- 4 cups whole wheat flour (*atta*)
- 1¼ cups milk, approx.
- 6 tbsp *desi ghee* or white butter
- 1 tsp salt
- 2 tbsp sugar
- 2 tsp dry yeast
- 4 tbsp screwpine flower water (*kewra water*)

METHOD

1. Warm 1¼ cups milk. Do not boil, just make it slightly warm. Dissolve sugar and yeast in warm milk. Add screwpine flower water. Cover and keep aside.
2. Add salt and *ghee* to flour and mix till it gets crumbly. Knead with milk to make medium soft dough. Cover with a damp cloth and set aside for 2-3 hours.
3. Divide the dough in 12 equal portions. Take one portion and roll into a ball. Dust with flour and roll out to a slightly thick round of about 6" diameter. Prick with a fork all over, leaving a margin of one inch on the sides.
4. Place the *sheermal* on a pre-heated *tawa* and cook it first on one side and then the other, until both sides are a rich golden brown. Alternatively, pre-heat oven to 350°F/180°C, place the *sheermals* on a greased tray and bake for about 15 minutes or till rich golden brown and cooked on both sides.

Khubani ka Mitha

Pulp of apricot with cream. Traditionally the light brown apricots with the seed are used. The kernel of the seed is used as the garnish for the dessert. Here we have used the orange, seedless variety of apricots to make the pulp and garnished with blanched and slivered almonds.

Serves 8-10

INGREDIENTS

- ½ kg dried apricot (*khubani*)
- ¾ cup (150 gms) sugar, or to taste
- 250 gm fresh cream

GARNISH

- almonds

METHOD

1. Soak apricots overnight with ¼ cup sugar in 2 cups water to cover them.
2. Next morning, boil apricots in the same water till tender. Remove seeds if present.
3. Sieve till only the fibre remains in the strainer.
4. Add a little water, the remaining sugar and cook till you get the consistency of custard. Garnish the dish with almonds. Serve with fresh cream.

taste of Tamil Nadu

Tamil Nadu is a land of varied beauty, with rocky mountains, dense forests, fertile plains of the Cauvery river, some arid regions, and a long coast line.

Tamil Nadu cuisine, traditionally vegetarian, is rice based. Rice is combined with lentils to make a light, fermented batter for dosas, idlis, and uttapams. Vadas are made from a batter of lentils only. Pongol consist of mashed rice and lentils, boiled together and seasoned with nuts, spices and ghee.

Sambar (dal), rasam (tamarind dal) and a great variety of curried vegetables, coconut and other chutneys, and pachadis (yogurt-based) are part of a typical meal. The food is much hotter and the curries and lentils are generally more soupy than their north Indian counterparts.

Chettinad is a small, arid area in southern Tamil Nadu. This is the home of the Chettiars who were a prosperous money lending and trading community and travelled abroad for business in the 19th and early 20th century. Nowadays this rural region is off the beaten track although it has the most amazing, opulent mansions using imported marble, Belgian glass and Burma teakwood, still standing from the past, worthy of museum status. The fame of its cuisine has spread far and wide – the dishes are hot and spicy, made with freshly ground masalas and a generous use of tamarind. Sun-dried vegetables are kept for use when fresh produce is in short supply. Chettinad cuisine offers a variety of vegetarian and non-vegetarian fare. Chettinad Pepper Chicken is by far the most famous.

The Minakshi Temple

Kurma Kuzhambu

A hot and spicy curry made with freshly ground green chillies and spices.

Serves 4

INGREDIENTS

- 1 potato, 1 carrot
- 1 *gaanth gobi* or knol-khol
- 10-12 french beans
- ½ cup shelled peas
- ½ small cauliflower
- 2 tbsp oil
- 1-2 tsp *ghee*
- 3-4 green chillies - slit
- 2 sprigs curry leaves
- 2 onions - chopped
- 2 tomatoes- chopped
- ½ tsp turmeric powder (*haldi*)
- ½-1 tsp chilli powder, or to taste
- 2 tsp coriander powder
- 1 tsp salt to taste

GRIND TO PASTE

- 1" piece ginger
- 6-8 flakes garlic
- 2-3 green chillies

GRIND SEPARATELY

- 6-8 tbsp coconut gratings
- 6-8 cashew nuts
- 3 tsp poppy seeds (*khus-khus*)
- 1 tbsp chopped coriander

SEASONINGS

- 2 bay leaves (*tej patta*)
- 6 cloves (*laung*)
- 3-4 large cardamoms (*moti elaichi*)
- 2 tsp aniseeds (*saunf*)

METHOD

1. Wash, peel and cut potato, carrot and knol-khol into small pieces of desired size. String and cut beans, break cauliflower into small florets. Steam or cook all the vegetables with just enough water, adding some salt.
2. Heat oil-*ghee* together, add seasonings and when done, add slit chillies, curry leaves and chopped onions. Fry till onions are brown.
3. Add ginger-garlic-green chilli paste and sauté on low heat for sometime.
4. Now add chopped tomato and continue to fry till they turn soft adding all the *masala* powders one at a time, stirring all the while, till oil surfaces.
5. Now add the vegetables, fry for 3-5 minutes.
6. Add coconut paste and fry for a minute. Add 1½ cups water, mix, cover and cook on low heat till the gravy is well blended. Remove from heat, pour into a bowl.
7. Garnish with chopped coriander leaves and fried cashew nuts. Serve hot with *puris,* plain rice or *aapam.*

Chicken Chettinad

Spicy, pepper flavoured chicken curry.

Serves 4-6

INGREDIENTS

- 1 chicken (700-800 gms) - cut into 12 pieces
- 5-6 tbsp oil
- 5-6 whole peppercorns
- 2 tsp chopped ginger
- 2 tsp chopped garlic
- 2 onions - chopped very finely
- ¼ cup curry leaves
- 3 tomatoes - pureed in a mixer
- 1 tsp salt, or to taste
- ¼ tsp turmeric (*haldi*) powder
- ¼ tsp chilli powder
- 2 tsp lemon juice

CHETTINAD MASALA

- 1 tbsp oil
- 1 tbsp poppy seeds (*khus-khus*)
- 6 tbsp freshly grated coconut (remove brown skin before grating)
- 1 tsp coriander seeds (*sabut dhania*)
- 1 tsp fennel seeds (*saunf*)
- ½ tsp cumin seeds (*jeera*)
- 1½ tsp peppercorns (*sabut kali mirch*)
- 5-6 whole, dry red chillies
- 3 green cardamoms (*chhoti elaichi*)
- 2-3 cloves (*laung*)
- 1" cinnamon stick (*dalchini*)

METHOD

1. Heat 1 tbsp oil in a pan. Add all ingredients of chettinad masala. Stir-fry till fragrant. Remove from heat. Grind together the roasted *masala* with ginger and garlic in a mixer grinder to a very smooth paste with ¼ cup water. Keep aside.
2. Heat 5-6 tbsp oil in a *kadhai* and add 4-5 whole peppercorns and the curry leaves. Wait for a few seconds. Add chopped onions. Fry till golden brown. Add salt, turmeric and chilli powder. Stir till well browned.
3. Add the pureed tomatoes. Cook for 4-5 minutes till oil separates.
4. Add the chicken and cook for 8-10 minutes on medium heat.
5. Add the ground paste. Sauté for 2 minutes.
6. Add 3 cups hot water. Cover and cook for 5-7 minutes or till chicken is tender, stirring in between. Cook till the *masala* is thick. Keep aside till serving time.
7. At serving time, add a little lemon juice to the chicken. Keep on low heat, stirring continuously, till it boils. Serve garnished with coriander.

Tomato Chutney

Serves 4

INGREDIENTS

- 250 gms tomatoes - roughly chopped
- 4 tbsp oil
- ½ tsp mustard seeds
- 1 tsp cumin seeds
- 2-3 green chillies, chopped
- 3 dry red chillies
- a few curry leaves
- 8-10 big garlic flakes - chopped
- 1 tbsp roasted split bengal gram (*bhuni channa dal* or *bhuna channa*)
- ½ tsp coriander powder
- 1 tsp salt
- 1 tbsp thick tamarind pulp

TEMPERING

- 1 tbsp oil
- a pinch of mustard and cumin seeds
- a few curry leaves
- 2 dry red chillies

METHOD FOR TOMATO CHUTNEY

1. Heat oil, crackle mustard seeds, and cumin. Add all other ingredients, except the tempering ingredients. Sauté for 2-3 minutes.
2. Add chopped tomatoes, sauté for 5 minutes. Remove from fire. Cool and grind to a rough paste.
3. For tempering, heat oil. Add mustard seeds, cumin seeds, red chillies and curry leaves. Stir and pour over the *chutney*.

Tamarind Rice

Rice flavoured with a special blend of spices. Peanuts add the desired crunch.

Serves 4

INGREDIENTS

- 1 cup rice - boiled in 6-7 cups water with 1 tsp salt and drained
- 1-2 tbsp oil to sprinkle
- 1 walnut size ball tamarind
- ½ cup grated dry coconut (*copra*)
- ¼ cup + 1 tbsp gingely oil (*til* oil)
- 1 tsp mustard seeds (*rai*)
- 2 pinches asafoetida (*hing*)
- 2 dry red chillies
- ¾ tsp salt or to taste
- ½ tsp turmeric powder
- 1 tbsp bengal gram *dal* (*channa dal*)
- 1 tbsp black gram *dal* (*urad dal*)
- 2 sprigs curry leaves
- ¼ cup roasted peanuts

DRY ROAST AND POWDER

- 1 tsp coriander seeds (*sabut dhania*)
- ½ tsp fenugreek seeds (*methi dana*)
- ½ tsp pepper corns (*sabut kali mirch*)
- ½ tsp cumin seeds (*jeera*)
- ¼ cup peanuts (*moongphali*)

DRY ROAST AND POWDER SEPARATELY

- ½ cup sesame seeds (*til*)

METHOD

1. Boil rice. Spread the cooked rice on a plate, sprinkle some oil and mix with a fork. Cover lightly and keep aside.
2. Boil tamarind in water, take out thick extract, about ½ cup pulp. Strain, keep aside.
3. Heat ¼ cup oil, add ½ tsp mustard seeds, a pinch of asafoetida, red chillies (broken into 2-3 pieces each). When mustard splutters, add tamarind water, salt and simmer on low heat till a thick *chutney* consistency is formed.
4. Heat 1 tbsp gingely oil or regular cooking oil in a *kadhai*, add ½ tsp mustard seeds, a pinch of asafoetida. When done, add bengal gram *dal*, black gram *dal* and curry leaves.
5. When *dals* turn brown, add the tamarind *chutney,* turmeric and freshly prepared powders. Add grated coconut and simmer for 3-5 minutes till oil surfaces.
6. Add roasted peanuts. Mix.
7. Add rice and mix well for 1-2 minutes.

taste of Karnataka

Karnataka is situated on the Deccan plateau and has a coastline on the Arabian Sea. The misty mountains of the Western Ghats have great scenic beauty – forests of teak, ebony and rosewood, dancing waterfalls and rich flora and fauna. The dish most often associated with this region is Bisi Bele Bhath, which simply means 'hot dal and rice', though it also includes all sorts of vegetables to make a complete meal. An every present street food and household snack is the Spicy Puffed Rice. Every district in Karnatak has christened it with its own name and given it slight variations.

In Mangalore, the food is generally spicy and rice based. Fresh coconut and chillies are important ingredients. Patrode is steamed stuffed colocasia leaves, a specialty worth tasting. Kori Gassi, Mangalorean Coconut Chilli Chicken Curry, and Kori Sukkha, Mangalorean Chicken with Coconut and Tamarind are among the signature dishes.

Udupi cuisine is strictly vegetarian. It is the original home of the popular Masala Dosa.

Famous desserts are Kesari bhath (a halwa made of semolina, sugar, and saffron), chiroti (a light flaky pastry sprinkled with granulated sugar and soaked in almond milk), and Mysore pak, made from gramflour, ghee, sugar and cardamom.

Bharatnatyam Dance.

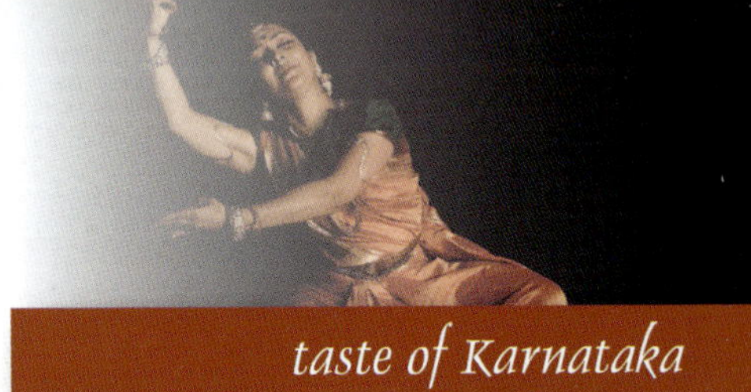

Masala Poori

Every household snack - spicy puffed rice!

Serves 4

INGREDIENTS

- 4 cups *poori* (puffed rice)
- ½ cup roasted ground nuts
- ½ tsp chilli powder
- ½ tsp turmeric powder
- 1 tsp mustard seeds
- ½ tsp asafoetida (*hing*)
- few curry leaves
- 3 green chillies - cut into thin long pieces
- 1 tbsp oil
- 1 tsp salt or to taste
- 10-12 thin slices of dry coconut (*copra*) - use a vegetable peeler to get thin slices (optional)

METHOD

1. Dry roast coconut pieces in a pan for a minute. Keep aside.
2. Heat oil in a *kadhai*, add mustard seeds, asafoetida, curry leaves and green chillies. Cook for 2 minutes.
3. Add ground nuts, chilli powder and turmeric powder. Wait for a minute.
4. Add puffed rice and salt. Mix well. Cook for 2- 3 minutes.
5. Add roasted coconut pieces to the above mixture, mix. Serve.

Kori Sukkha

Mangalorean Chicken with Coconut and Tamarind

Serves 4

INGREDIENTS

- 800 gms chicken (8 medium sized pieces)
- 5-6 tbsp *ghee*/butter/oil
- few curry leaves
- ½ tsp turmeric
- 1 tbsp tamarind paste
- 1 onion - finely chopped

GARNISH

- 1 onion - sliced thinly and fried till golden brown

PASTE 1 - INGREDIENTS (ROAST & GRIND)

- 1 tsp black pepper
- ½ tsp fennel seeds (*saunf*)
- 1 tbsp poppy seeds (*khus-khus*)
- 10-12 dry, red chillies
- 2 tbsp coriander seeds (*sabut dhania*)
- a pinch fenugreek seeds (*methi dana*)
- 1 tsp cumin (*jeera*)

PASTE 2 - INGREDIENTS

- 12 garlic flakes
- 2 tsp salt
- 1 medium sized coconut - grated

METHOD

1. Roast paste 1 ingredients for 2-3 minutes in a pan till fragrant. Add onion, turmeric and tamarind paste. Grind all together without water to a smooth paste.
2. Coarsely grind ingredients for paste 2 separately without adding water.
3. Heat 5-6 tbsp oil. Add curry leaves and paste 1 and stir for 3-4 minutes. Add chicken pieces and stir for 2-3 minutes. Cover and cook for 10 minutes till almost done.
4. Add second paste, cook covered for 5-7 minutes till tender. Garnish with fried onions.

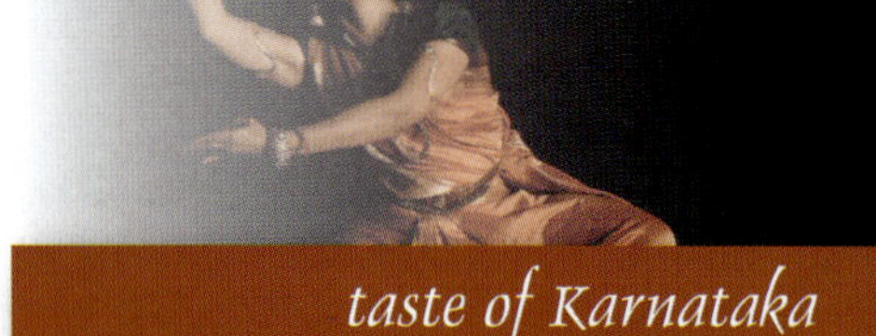

taste of Karnataka

Kori Gassi

A Mangalorean coconut and chilli chicken curry.

Serves 4

MARINATE TOGETHER

- 1 kg chicken - cut into 8 pieces
- ½ tsp turmeric powder
- 1 tsp salt

OTHER INGREDIENTS

- 250 gm grated coconut
- 2 tsp chopped garlic
- 2-3 onions - chopped
- 6 dry, red chillies
- 2 tsp coriander seeds (*sabut dhania*)
- 1½ tsp peppercorns (*sabut kali mirch*)
- 1 tsp cumin seeds (*jeera*)
- ¼ tsp fenugreek seeds (*methi dana*)
- ½ cup groundnut oil
- 2 tbsp tamarind pulp
- 1 tsp salt
- ¼ tsp turmeric powder

METHOD

1. Marinate chicken with salt and turmeric and keep aside.
2. Heat 1 tbsp oil in a frying pan, add red chillies, coriander seeds, peppercorns, fenugreek seeds, cumin seeds and roast on medium heat until golden brown. Remove spices and cool.
3. Put coconut and garlic in a grinder, add the roasted spices. Grind to make a very fine paste, using a little water. Keep aside.
4. Heat oil in handi, add onions and sauté over medium heat until golden brown.
5. Add the ground paste, 1 tsp salt and ¼ tsp turmeric powder. Stir fry for 5 minutes. Add about 2 cups water and bring to a boil.
6. Add chicken and simmer until the chicken is cooked.
7. Add tamarind pulp and continue cooking for 5 minutes. Adjust the seasoning. Garnish with chopped coriander leaves.

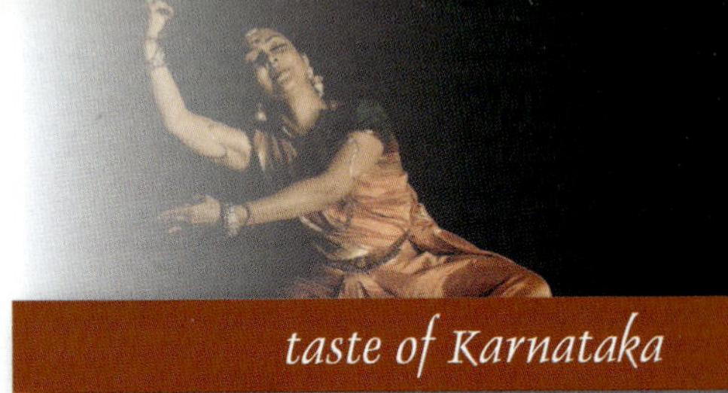

taste of Karnataka

Bisi Bele Bhath

Rice cooked with vegetables added lentils, make it a complete meal.

Serves 4-6

INGREDIENTS

- 1 cup rice
- 1 cup *arhar dal* - soaked for 15 minutes
- 1 small carrot - cut into small pieces
- 1 potato - cut into small pieces
- 5-6 beans - cut into small pieces
- 1 long, thin brinjal - cut into small pieces
- 1 drumstick - cut into small pieces
- 5-6 tbsp oil
- a pinch asafoetida (*hing*)
- 1 tsp mustard seeds (*sarson*)
- 2-3 dry red chillies
- 15-20 curry leaves
- 2 green chillies - cut into small pieces
- 1 large onion - cut into small pieces
- a pinch of turmeric (*haldi*) powder
- 2 lemon size tamarind (*imli*) soaked in ¾ cup water - strained to get 1 cup pulp
- 2 tsp sugar or jaggery (gur)

BISI BELE PASTE

- 2 tbsp *channa dal*
- 2 tbsp *dhuli urad dal*
- pinch of asafoetida (*hing*)
- 2 tbsp coriander seeds (*sabut dhania*)
- 4-6 dry red chillies
- 1 tsp cumin seeds (*jeera*)
- 1 tsp fenugreek seeds (*methi dana*)
- 1 tsp mustard seeds (*rai*)
- 4 black peppercorns (*sabut kali mirch*)
- 2 sticks cinnamon (*dalchini*)
- 2 tbsp dried grated coconut (*copra*)

TOPPING

- 1 tbsp *ghee*
- a few curry leaves

METHOD

1. To make the *Bisi bele* paste, heat a pan and dry roast *channa* and *urad dal* till brown. Remove from heat. In the same pan add 1 tsp oil and add asafoetida, coriander seeds, cumin seeds, mustard seeds, fenugreek seeds, black pepper, red chillies and cinnamon. Cook till cumin seeds and fenugreek turn light brown, add coconut and stir for ½ minute. Remove from heat. Place the roasted *dals* in a grinder and grind to a smooth powder, now add the rest of the roasted ingredients in the grinder and grind all using about ½ cup water to get a smooth paste.
2. For the *bhath,* add rice, dal and 6 cups of water in a pressure cooker. Add 3 tsp salt and pressure cook to 1 whistle. Lower heat and cook for 3-4 minutes. Remove from heat and let the pressure drop by itself.
3. Heat oil in *kadhai,* add a pinch of asafoetida, add mustard seeds, broken red chillies, curry leaves and green chillies. Stir and add the onions. Cook till slightly soft. Add the vegetables and lower heat. Cover and cook for about 10 minutes or till vegetables are soft, add a pinch of turmeric and the *Bisi bele* paste. Stir well. Remove from heat.
4. Open the cooker, add the vegetables to the cooked rice-*dal* mixture, mix lightly.
5. Mash the soaked *imli* and strain to get a puree, add to the *bhath* and mix. Add sugar.
6. Add *ghee* and fresh curry *patta.* Serve hot with potato chips or *khara boondi* (fried *masala boondi*) or *raita.*

SWIFT

taste of Kerala

Kerala is a beautiful strip of coastal land, known for its luscious vegetation, lagoons and backwaters. The link with geography and history is plainly evident in the cuisine of Kerala. The climate is ideal for rice cultivation. Coconuts and bananas grow everywhere in this region and are used generously in the cooking. Kerala's long coast line, its numerous rivers and back waters, provide fish and seafood of all kind.

Over the centuries the deep harbours of Kerala have received ocean-going ships and their visitors from faraway places – China, Europe and the Arab world –who came for commerce, particularly for spices, and left their mark on the culture and cuisine of the region. Muslims brought in a spicy version of biryani and other meat and chicken dishes. Syrian Christians introduced new ways of cooking fish for example meen pollichathu and fish molee, and new desserts such a crunchy kozhalappam, achappam, cheeda, churuttu etc. From neighbouring Tamil-speaking areas they adopted idli, dosa, rasam and sambar.

Appam, a fermented flat bread, is made of rice flour and coconut. It has become the identity of all Keralites, wherever they live. The local fermenting agent is toddy but today more people use yeast or other quick methods of making appams light and airy.

The famous Snake Boat race.

Appam with Vegetable Stew

Appams from Kerala are light and airy pancakes, white on top and golden underneath. The process of making them starts by soaking rice and urad dal, then grinding it to a coarse paste with coconut water and allowing it to ferment overnight. Learn to make them perfectly every time in these step-by-step instructions. Serve them with Vegetable Stew.

Makes 6

INGREDIENTS - for APPAM

- 1 cup raw rice - *permal* rice
- ¼ cup urad dal
- 1 cup coconut water
- ½ tsp salt
- ½ tsp sugar
- ½ tsp baking soda (*mitha soda*)
- ½ cup coconut milk
- ¾ tsp eno fruit salt, optional
- 6" *appam* wok or a small non-stick pan

METHOD

1. Clean, wash and soak the rice and urad dal for 3 hours. Grind to a paste (not very fine), adding coconut water as required to get a thick pouring consistency. Add salt, sugar and soda, stir well. Cover and keep overnight to ferment. Do not put it in a cupboard or a warm place for fermentation.
2. At serving time, add coconut milk to the batter to get a thin pouring consistency which coats the back of a laddle (*kadchhi*). If needed add ¼-1/3 cup water to thin down the batter.
3. Heat a small nonstick fry pan or an *appam kadhai* (*chatti*) and brush with a little oil.
4. Add eno fruit salt to the batter and mix well. Remove *chatti* from heat. Add about ¾ ladle full of the batter in the centre of the *kadhai* and swirl immediately taking it upto the sides nicely. Do not spread the batter with the *kadchhi*, else all the holes will get blocked.
5. Cover and cook over low heat for 2-3 minutes till the edges turn crisp, while the centre is soft and spongy. The top is whitish but the underside is light golden. Serve with stew.

INGREDIENTS - for VEGETABLE STEW

- 1 carrot - cut into small cubes
- 10 french beans - cut into ½" pieces
- ½ cup shelled peas
- 1 small potato - cut into small cubes
- ½ cup small florets of cauliflower
- 2 sprigs curry leaves
- 3-4 green chillies - slit
- 2 medium size onions - chopped
- 1 tsp ginger paste
- 1 tsp garlic paste
- 1¼ tsp salt, or to taste
- ½-1 tsp chilli powder, optional
- 2½ cups coconut milk
- 1½ tbsp cornflour
- 2 tbsp chopped coriander
- ½ tsp *garam masala*
- ¼ tsp crushed pepper

TEMPERING

- 2 tbsp oil
- 2 bay leaves (*tej patta*)
- ½ tsp mustard seeds (*sarson*)
- 4 cloves (*laung*)
- 2 cinnamon pieces
- 3 black cardamoms (*moti elaichi*)
- ½ tsp pepper corns (*sabut kali mirch*)

METHOD FOR VEGETABLE STEW

1. Heat oil, add all ingredients of tempering and wait till fragrant, about a minute.
2. Add curry leaves, slit chillies and onions. Sauté onions lightly till translucent and start to change colour, do not allow them to get brown.
3. Add ginger-garlic pastes, fry for a minute.
4. Add vegetables, stir fry for a while. When they get slightly soft, after about 3-4 minutes, add salt, chilli powder and ½ cup coconut milk mixed with ½ cup water and 1 tbsp cornflour. Cover and cook on low heat till the vegetables are done and the liquid has almost dried up.
5. Add the remaining coconut milk, chopped coriander, *garam masala* and crushed pepper. If it appears thick, add about ½ cup hot water. Boil for 2-3 minutes. Remove from heat. Check salt and *masalas*. Serve with *appam.*

Note: You can blanch or steam the vegetables if you like before cooking.

A thin coconut and yogurt based curry, tempered with coconut oil.

Serves 4

INGREDIENTS

- 1 raw banana
- 1 small carrot
- 4 beans
- 2 small drumsticks
- 1 small potato or 100 gms yam
- 1 tsp salt
- ¼ tsp turmeric (*haldi*) powder

TEMPERING

- 2 tbsp coconut oil
- ½ tsp mustard seeds (*sarson*)
- few curry leaves
- 2 dry red chillies

PASTE

- ½ fresh coconut - grated
- 1 tsp cumin seeds (*jeera*)
- 3-4 green chillies
- ¾ cup yogurt
- 2 tsp rice powder

METHOD

1. Cut raw banana, carrot, beans drumsticks, and potato into 1" long pieces. Boil 4-5 cups water. Add 1 tsp salt and ¼ tsp turmeric. Add vegetables. Boil for 2 minutes till slightly soft. Drain and keep aside.
2. Grind all ingredients of the paste till smooth.
3. Add 1½ cups water to the paste and keep on low heat, stirring continuously till it boils.
4. Add vegetables and simmer for a minute. Remove the *avial* from heat.
5. Heat 2 tbsp coconut oil. Add mustard seeds. Reduce heat. Add curry leaves and red chillies. Pour tempering on the *avial.* Serve hot.

A dry dish of shredded cabbage with coconut.

Serves 4

INGREDIENTS

- 500 gms cabbage - chopped
- 2 tbsp coconut oil
- ½ tsp mustard seeds
- 1 tsp *urad dal*
- 4 dry red chillies - cut into 2-3 pieces
- ¼ tsp turmeric powder
- ¼ tsp red chilli powder, 1 tsp salt

GRIND TO A PASTE

- 1 cup grated coconut
- ¼ tsp cumin
- 1 green chilli
- 2 sprigs curry leaves
- 2 garlic flakes

METHOD

1. Heat oil, add mustard seeds, *urad dal,* dry red chillies. Let the *dal* turn golden.
2. Add cabbage, mix well and cook covered for 7-8 minutes and keep aside.
3. Add freshly ground coconut paste, turmeric powder, chilli powder, salt to cabbage. Cook without covering for 2 minutes. Serve hot.

Karimeen

Spicy, whole pamfret wrapped in a banana leaf and cooked to perfection in the oven.

Serves 2-3

INGREDIENTS

- 1 fish (pearl spot/pomfret) (400 gms) - clean and slit on both sides
- 3 tbsp grated fresh coconut
- ¼ tsp black pepper
- 2 tbsp coriander powder
- ¼ tsp turmeric powder
- 1 tbsp chilli powder
- 4 tbsp oil
- 1-2 green chillies
- ½ tsp ginger paste
- ½ tsp garlic paste
- 1-2 tbsp vinegar
- 1 tsp salt or to taste
- 5-6 curry leaves
- ¼ piece banana leaf

METHOD

1. Dry roast grated coconut, black pepper, coriander powder, turmeric powder and chilli powder on a *tawa*. Keep aside.
2. Grind the dry roasted above ingredients with oil, green chillies, ginger paste, garlic paste, vinegar, salt curry leaves and 1-2 tbsp of water to a fine paste.
3. Apply the *masala* to the fish on both the sides.
4. Apply oil to the banana leaf and wrap the fish with the oil side touching the fish. Bake for 15 minutes at 180°C.

Malabar Parotha

A flaky parantha from the Malabar coast of Kerala.

Makes 6

INGREDIENTS

- 450 gms flour (*maida*)
- a pinch of baking soda
- 2 eggs, 1 cup milk, approx.
- 1 tsp salt, 2½ tsp sugar
- 4 tbsp oil, 6 tbsp melted butter
- *ghee* to shallow fry

METHOD

1. Sieve flour with baking soda into a *paraat.*
2. In a bowl, whisk together - eggs, milk, sugar, salt and oil.
3. Make a bay in the flour, pour the egg and milk mixture in it and knead to a soft dough using some more milk if needed. Cover with a moist cloth and keep aside for 30 min.
4. Divide the dough into 6 equal portions and make balls. Flatten each with a rolling pin into a round of a *chapati* size. Grease the work-surface lightly and place the *chapati* on it. Stretch evenly on all sides, until it is very thin (approx 15" diameter).
5. Apply melted butter over the entire surface, dust with flour, pleat the *roti* so as to get a strip with many folds. Twist the strip lightly. Roll the strip to make a *pedha* and then flatten slightly. Keep aside covered for 5 minutes. Flatten each *pedha* with a rolling pin into a round *parantha* size (approx 9" diameter), dusting with flour while rolling.
6. Cook *parantha* on a heated *tawa* till half done on both sides. Pour *ghee* all round and shallow fry both sides over low heat until golden brown.

international conversion guide

These are not exact equivalents; they've been rounded-off to make measuring easier.

WEIGHTS & MEASURES

METRIC	IMPERIAL
15 g	½ oz
30 g	1 oz
60 g	2 oz
90 g	3 oz
125 g	4 oz (¼ lb)
155 g	5 oz
185 g	6 oz
220 g	7 oz
250 g	8 oz (½ lb)
280 g	9 oz
315 g	10 oz
345 g	11 oz
375 g	12 oz (¾ lb)
410 g	13 oz
440 g	14 oz
470 g	15 oz
500 g	16 oz (1 lb)
750 g	24 oz (1 ½ lb)
1 kg	30 oz (2 lb)

LIQUID MEASURES

METRIC	IMPERIAL
30 ml	1 fluid oz
60 ml	2 fluid oz
100 ml	3 fluid oz
125 ml	4 fluid oz
150 ml	5 fluid oz (¼ pint/1 gill)
190 ml	6 fluid oz
250 ml	8 fluid oz
300 ml	10 fluid oz (½ pint)
500 ml	16 fluid oz
600 ml	20 fluid oz (1 pint)
1000 ml	1¾ pints

CUPS & SPOON MEASURES

METRIC	IMPERIAL
1 ml	¼ tsp
2 ml	½ tsp
5 ml	1 tsp
15 ml	1 tbsp
60 ml	¼ cup
125 ml	½ cup
250 ml	1 cup

HELPFUL MEASURES

METRIC	IMPERIAL
3 mm	1/8 in
6 mm	¼ in
1 cm	½ in
2 cm	¾ in
2.5 cm	1 in
5 cm	2 in
6 cm	2½ in
8 cm	3 in
10 cm	4 in
13 cm	5 in
15 cm	6 in
18 cm	7 in
20 cm	8 in
23 cm	9 in
25 cm	10 in
28 cm	11 in
30 cm	12 in (1 ft)

HOW TO MEASURE

When using the graduated metric measuring cups, it is important to shake the dry ingredients loosely into the required cup. Do not tap the cup on the table, or pack the ingredients into the cup unless otherwise directed. Level top of cup with a knife. When using graduated metric measuring spoons, level top of spoon with a knife. When measuring liquids in the jug, place jug on a flat surface, check for accuracy at eye level.

OVEN TEMPERATURE

These oven temperatures are only a guide. Always check the manufacturer's manual.

	°C (*Celsius*)	°F (*Fahrenheit*)	Gas Mark
Very Low	120	250	1
Low	150	300	2
Moderately Low	160	325	3
Moderate	180	350	4
Moderately High	190	375	5
High	200	400	6
Very High	230	450	7

glossary of herbs and spices

ENGLISH NAME	HINDI NAME
Asafoetida	Hing
Bay Leaves	Tej Patta
Cardamom	Elaichi, Chhoti Elaichi
Cardamom, Black	Moti Elaichi
Carom Seeds	Ajwain
Chillies, Green	Hari Mirch
Chillies, Dry Red	Sukhi Sabut Lal Mirch
Chilli Powder, Red	Lal Mirch Powder
Cinnamon	Dalchini
Cloves	Laung
Coriander Seeds	Sabut Dhania
Coriander Seeds, ground	Dhania Powder
Coriander Leaves	Hara Dhania
Cumin Seeds	Jeera
Cumin Seeds, black	Shah Jeera
Curry Leaves	Kari Patta
Fennel Seeds	Saunf
Fenugreek Seeds	Methi Dana
Fenugreek Leaves, Dried	Kasuri Methi
Garam Masala Powder	Garam Masala
Garlic	Lahsun
Ginger	Adrak
Mace	Javitri
Mango Powder, Dried	Amchoor
Melon Seeds	Magaz
Mint Leaves	Pudina
Mustard Seeds	Rai, Sarson
Nigella, Onion Seeds	Kalaunji
Nutmeg	Jaiphal
Peppercorns	Sabut Kali Mirch
Pomegranate Seeds, Dried	Anardana
Sesame Seeds	Til
Saffron	Kesar
Turmeric Powder	Haldi

glossary of regional cuisines of India

MILK PRODUCTS

Malai – layers of thick spongy cream on boiled and cooled milk
Khoya, mawa – reduced dried milk sold in lumps
Rabri – whole milk is cooked until it is clotted and thick
Paneer – block cottage cheese
Curd – yogurt, *dahi*
Hung yogurt – well drained thick yogurt
Kulfi – Indian ice cream with a dense texture

LENTILS

Green moong dal, whole - sabut moong
Green moong dal, split - moong tukda
Yellow moong dal (green skin fully removed) - dhuli moong
Black urad dal - sabut urad
White urad dal (black skin fully removed) - dhuli urad
Arhar dal – flat, bright yellow dal
Channa dal – rounded, yellow, nutty flavour
Kala channa - small chick peas with dark skins

FLOURS

Whole wheat flour - *atta*
Millet flour - *atta* of *bajra*
Maize flour - *atta* of *makki*
Gram flour - *besan*

EQUIPMENT and METHOD

Kadhai – Indian wok
tawa – griddle
Bhunna – slow stir-frying on low heat till the water content is reduced
Dhungar – adding a smoke flavour to food

MISCELLANIES

Amrud – guava
Achaar – pickle
Bhindi – lady fingers, okra
Ghee – clarified butter
Jaggery – raw brown sugar, *gur*
Jhinga – prawns
Kachri – used as a meat tenderiser
Maans – local word for meat, mutton
Kairi – mango, raw, green
Kukkad – local word for chicken
Mangodi – ready-made small balls made from spiced lentil paste
Matar – green peas
Murg – chicken
Palak – spinach
Papaya paste – raw papaya used as a meat tenderiser
Pyaz – onion
Salt, black – reddish-black crystals with distinct sharp taste
Salt, rock – natural, unrefined salt, in crystalline chunks
Soda-bi-carb – *mitha* soda - baking soda

NAMES OF TYPICAL DISHES

Bada, vada – a deep-fried snack made from various batters
Bharta – any dish with coarsely mashed, seasoned vegetables
Bharwan – a vegetable that is stuffed with any filling
Chilla – pancake made from lentil batter
Kachori – flaky, deep-fried bread with various fillings
Kachumbar salad – diced cucumber, tomato, onion with seasoning and lemon juice
Khichri – rice/wheat/millet cooked with lentils to make a soft (not soupy) dish
Launji – any sweet and spicy chutney
Panna – a summer drink with raw mangos
Kanji – an appetiser soaked in spicy liquid
Subzi – any vegetarian dish made with vegetables or other vegetarian ingredient
Sula – traditional barbecue
Gatte – rolls made of gram flour dough